Life Insurance for the
American Family

Life Insurance for the American Family

✦

Most of What You Know About Life Insurance is Wrong

Ed Kelly

iUniverse, Inc.

New York Bloomington Shanghai

Life Insurance for the American Family
Most of What You Know About Life Insurance is Wrong

iUniverse books may be ordered through booksellers or by contacting:

iUniverse
1663 Liberty Drive
Bloomington, IN 47403
www.iuniverse.com
1-800-Authors (1-800-288-4677)

Because of the dynamic nature of the Internet, any Web addresses or links contained in this book may have changed since publication and may no longer be valid.

The information, ideas, and suggestions in this book are not intended to render professional advice. Before following any suggestions contained in this book, you should consult your personal accountant or other financial advisor. Neither the author nor the publisher shall be liable or responsible for any loss or damage allegedly arising as a consequence of your use or application of any information or suggestions in this book.

ISBN: 978-0-595-46742-6 (pbk)
ISBN: 978-0-595-91037-3 (ebk)

Printed in the United States of America

Contents

Acknowledgments

I wish to acknowledge and thank all of the following:

Valerie, Stephen and Shannon…my family and my inspiration.
Roy Geer, mentor, coach, and protector of the vision.
Gary Grossman, Mike Haglin, John Scarbrough, and Curt Sorensen, primary movers.
Rhonda Marks, editor, guide, and voice of reason.

For contributions in many forms: Jim, Bobby, George, Mickey, BJ, Caleb, Gayle, Todd, Robin, Rich, John, Tim, Paul, Doug, Jerry, Rick, Brent, Bob, Gail, Greg, Stacey, Vicky and especially, Patty.
To other authors and guides: Ben Baldwin, Ed Slott, Barry Kaye, Stephen Covey, Viktor Frankl, John Allen, Ayn Rand, Frederich Hayek, Thomas Sowell, Henry Hazlett, Mark Helprin, George Washington and of course, Thomas Jefferson
Thank you to the many others who have contributed to my life and to my work.

This book is dedicated to all who work for and fight for individual freedom throughout the world.

Introduction

When I began my career as a financial adviser in 1986, my first client was my mom. In my first few weeks in the profession, I didn't know much about financial products or anything else so I turned to my manager for his recommendations on my mom's financial plan. One of the recommendations he made was a life insurance policy.

Over the next couple of years, as my industry knowledge expanded, I came to suspect that the policy was implemented more for my manager's production goals than for my mother's benefit. After all, why should my mother, a widow with all her kids grown, "need" insurance of this kind? The situation smelled bad to me.

But when Mom died in the sixth year of the policy, the $35,000 premium (paid in a single lump sum) proved to be a smart financial decision when a $100,000 tax-free payment was made to our family. When I deposited the check, I cried both in grief at the loss of my mother and in gratitude for an invaluable financial planning lesson learned: Money invested in an insurance policy can, and most often does, have a high return on investment.

I share my story because, probably like you, I have been skeptical about life insurance. Like most consumers, the information that I had been given about life insurance was flawed. Over the past two decades, however, I have come to see life insurance in a different light—as a critical component of solid financial planning. My perspective has been informed through study and more important, through witnessing the benefits bestowed on many of the people my colleagues and I have advised. I offer my perspective to you here in this book through some of the real-life stories that illustrate the potential benefits of life insurance as well as the potential hazards of being grossly underinsured.

The objective of this book is simple: to move you (and those counting on you) from shaky to solid financial ground—from being underinsured to being properly insured. This book will help you discover (1) why you are grossly underinsured, (2) what your best options are for dealing with that reality, and (3) where to go for help in remedying your current situation.

This is not a self-help book. The decisions required of you in this aspect of your overall financial plan are too crucial to make without expert guidance. This book offers several valuable assists as you work with your advisers toward a bright and sure-footed financial future. First, this book defines the terminology surrounding the topic of life insurance, which is available in a number of forms or products. Each product is described in sidebars as they are first mentioned in the main text. For convenience, the descriptions (and other industry terms) also appear in the Glossary of Life Insurance Terminology at the end of the book. Second, this book provides a conceptual framework for decision-making—explaining the issues, dispelling the myths, and clearing away the smoke screens that confuse most consumers when contemplating life insurance. Finally, each chapter concludes with a simple set of questions designed to foster effective dialogue between you and your financial planning professionals as you go forward.

In reading this book, you will gain insights and formulate questions that will lead you, with the help of your advisers, to some smart choices about your own life insurance situation. Together, you will come up with great solutions to your current financially precarious situation that most likely finds you grossly underinsured.

With this book I wish for you and your family happiness, abundance, and peace of mind. That's my bottom line. Pretty simple.

Financial advice can be sought from a variety of professionals wearing different "hats" and bearing a myriad of titles. These financial services professionals include (but are not limited to) the following: insurance agents, registered representatives, financial advisers, stockbrokers, financial planners, wealth managers, estate planners, and tax attorneys. For simplicity, I use the generic term *advisers* throughout this book, except occasionally when I specify certain professions. Most financial services professionals are qualified to address the issues discussed in this book.

1

You Are Grossly Underinsured

You, dear reader, are grossly underinsured. I don't even know you, but I know this is true.

Industry statistics and my professional experience lead to this sad conclusion. Over 60% of Americans know they should have more life insurance. On average, however, Americans carry less than two times current annual income in life insurance coverage.

Think for a moment: How long could you survive on only two year's worth of your spouse's income in the event of his or her death?

Whether you are the head of a young family just beginning to plan your financial future or a family with an amassed wealth, you are likely to be dramatically underinsured—but for different reasons. The scenarios in the sidebars exemplify what I mean.

The force is against you here. There are just too many reasons that you don't buy the life insurance you should have. They range from your financial advisers' biases to your own tendencies toward instant gratification—tendencies that are a part of human nature. But that's another story. Let's look first at your advisers.

If your financial professionals are like most, they are biased toward underinsuring or disinclined even to mention life insurance for the following reasons:

- They personally own a small amount of coverage themselves—making it difficult to think of large face-value policies, possibly because they don't have as much financial worth as you.

- They are focused on money management rather than risk management. Most advisers find money management more fun than the tedium of life insurance.

- They may be like some insurance salespeople who admit to not even liking many types of life insurance, or they may feel "labeled" as insurance agents—the perceived stigma preventing them from offering you sound advice. Industry research continually shows that consumers *know* they need more life insurance, but few will actively go out and purchase it. If an insurance agent met with you and asked you to purchase more coverage, you probably would. But chances are you aren't being asked.

- Many financial professionals have moved to a "fee based" practice so that products like life insurance, which have commissions associated with them, tend not to be used by "fee only" advisers.

- They have a heightened sense of political correctness. They find it difficult to express a strong opinion about *anything,* much less about matters of death and life insurance, thus making them reticent to ask the questions necessary for underwriting a policy—questions about whether you have AIDS or ever smoked marijuana or other very personal information.

- They think and talk about life insurance only in terms of need— asking you only how much you need for survivor income rather than how much your life is worth in monetary terms. Fearing that you will balk at large-face-value policies, they opt to sell you a small policy rather than none at all.

- They have seen insurance policies that have not worked as planned. Based on those bad experiences, they have decided that they don't like insurance. This is illogical, because they also have seen investments sometimes not work out as planned and yet, despite those disappointing outcomes, they still agree to manage your money.

- They are inadequately licensed.[1] Many of the newer life insurance products require multiple licensing, including licenses to sell stock-oriented investment vehicles. Many insurance agents simply do not hold all the licenses required. Consequently, they cannot offer you the full range of options to meet all your needs and objectives.

- Finally, they simply do not understand all the products available (which change rapidly) or their appropriate value to clients.

---

1 Recent research shows that in just the last four years, financial advisers have moved from having 13% of their business based on insurance (the rest being investments and financial planning fees) to now just 1.6%. This finding illustrates the rapid move in the industry away from insurance advice and implementation. Pomering, R. (2006). Moss Adams & SEI Research.

Those are some of the reasons your advisers are not giving you the complete counsel you need about life insurance. Now, what about you? If you are like I was so many years ago, you simply don't want to spend money on life insurance. You would rather spend your money on something that provides immediate pleasure. You want to avoid the cost and the responsibility associated with life insurance. In fact, you want to avoid the topic altogether because the matter of life insurance deals with death—an unsettling subject indeed.

Also you may think that you already know a lot about life insurance—but how can you? For the reasons cited previously, your financial advisers have offered little or no guidance. And the media haven't been much help either. Most financial journalists insubstantially warn against being "overinsured." They tend to focus solely on cost and not on the broader issues at stake. And journalists seem to like easy targets—and insurance salesmen are easy targets.

Paul and Nicole's Story

Having recently changed jobs, Paul, age 32, wanted to roll over his 401(k), valued at $130,000, to an IRA account. His financial adviser was happy to provide options and advice for this transaction. In their initial and subsequent meetings, the adviser never raised the topic of life insurance with Paul and his wife, Nicole. Tragically, three years later, Paul was killed in an auto accident—leaving Nicole alone at age 28 to raise their 18-month-old child. Paul's group *term insurance* policy paid $75,000—the amount of "one times income." Additionally, his parents had purchased a $25,000 *whole life* policy when he was born. The insurance payouts, IRA funds, and about $160,000 in savings and other investments totaled about $390,000.

Within the first year following Paul's death, Nicole quit her part-time job because she was emotionally unable to focus on her work and her child. She could no longer afford part-time day care. With her funds rapidly depleting, the financial adviser calculated that Nicole would need to sell her house within 18 months and move into an apartment—stretching her dwindling funds over a few more years. Consequently, Nicole had to consider moving in with her parents, across the country, until she could recover emotionally and financially.

As this book will help you discover, however, it is impossible to be overinsured with life insurance. So let's move forward and put four facts (some of them unpleasant) on the table:

Fact #1: You are going to die some day.

If you are struggling with this one, this book cannot help you.

Fact #2: Life insurance is a tool, not a religion. Life insurance is just a financial tool—not a faith-based initiative. You don't need to "believe" in life insurance to know that you will die and that you are responsible for safeguarding your dependents against that inevitability. Moreover, because you know that you will die, you can use life insurance to accomplish many other financial goals beyond covering your survivors' needs in the event of your death. Indeed, life insurance is a great tool for building your financial "house." In later chapters, we'll look at the "rooms" you might build into your financial plan by using life insurance as a tool.

Fact #3: Insurance is a tool to be used throughout your entire life—and beyond. You probably think you need life insurance only when the kids are young—and that you certainly don't need life insurance when you are retired. Wrong. If you are struggling financially, you should have it. If you are very successful financially, you should have it. If you don't like taxes, you should have it. If someone depends on your income stream, you should have it. If you make a lot of money and think you are now self-insured, you probably should have a lot of it.

Fred and Marilyn's Story

Fred and Marilyn, both 71 years of age, perished in the 2004 tsunami while vacationing in Thailand. At the time of their deaths, the couple had accumulated a large estate with a net worth of about $10 million. Fred's 50% ownership in a manufacturing company was worth about $4 million. In addition, they owned an apartment building valued at $3 million, Fred's IRA rollover account valued at $2 million, their Laguna Beach condo, and miscellaneous investments and cash. One would think that Fred and Marilyn had left their heirs—their two children and six grandchildren—with no financial problems. But in fact, the heirs faced estate taxes totaling $2.5 million, which had to be paid within nine months. Where was the money going to come from? Fred's partner in the manufacturing company didn't have $4 million in cash to pay the heirs. And with the real estate market down, selling the apartment building was not a great option. That left only one option: liquidating the IRA account. But the heirs were forced to pay *income* tax on the money used to pay the estate tax owed. This double taxation devastated the liquid IRA account.

We humans can see only what we know to see. And it is difficult for us to see things that we haven't even imagined. As in our youth, we ponder what kind of job we might have when we grow up. We think of being a policeman or a teacher or a doctor or the President. Today, perhaps the idea is to grow up to be a winner on *American Idol* or a custom motorcycle builder or a video game programmer.

The point is that we tend to imagine our futures only in obvious terms. For example, it might not be obvious to you (yet) that upon reaching age 65, you might want insurance for *pension maximization strategies*. Nor might it be obvious to you at age 30 that you should think of creating liquid funds to "even out" the estate at the time of your death. (See Phil's story.) Nor might it be obvious to you at age 45 that you should consider having insurance so that, upon your death at age 87, you leave to your grandchildren tax-free, liquid dollars and leave to charity your taxable IRA (individual retirement account)—thereby avoiding taxation on that portion of the wealth you created during your lifetime.

A *pension maximization strategy* is used for retirees faced with choosing among various monthly pension options. They must decide whether to take a higher amount each month, leaving their spouses with nothing when they die, or a reduced monthly amount, leaving continuing pensions to their survivors. An alternative approach to a reduced pension is to use life insurance to replace the pension amount in the event of death. Sometimes the numbers work, sometimes they don't. How many consumers realize they may want life insurance at retirement for this purpose?

Phil's Story

My client Phil owned a printing business. As he approached retirement, his daughter, Melissa, took over increasing responsibilities managing the business. Phil's net worth was $3 million, with $2 million of that represented in the value of the business. Phil wanted Melissa to inherit the business upon his death. But he also wanted his son, Adam, to get an "equal share" of the estate. These wishes posed a dilemma since $2 million of Phil's worth was tied up in the business, leaving only $1 million in the balance. Through discussions with Phil's attorney, we mapped out a number of alternative approaches to this dilemma. Together, we decided on a simple solution: buying a million-dollar life insurance policy payable to Adam at the time of Phil's death. This measure had the effect of evening out Phil's estate and creating an equal share for both heirs.

There are a thousand reasons you might need or want to have insurance throughout your life. You just aren't aware of 998 of them (yet). In reading this book, you are raising your awareness.

Fact #4: There is a difference between the amount of insurance your family "needs" and the economic loss your eventual death represents.

The word *need* has the entire financial industry tripping all over itself. Need is like the fur ball the cat is choking on. Most advisers can't even talk about insurance without choking on the word. They speak of need amount—the amount of money that a family would require just to maintain a basic lifestyle in the event of a breadwinner's death.

But wait. Let's try taking another angle on the matter. For a moment, think about Bill Gates, founder of Microsoft, and his mansion on the shores of Lake Washington in the Seattle suburbs. Imagine Bill is in a meeting with his accountants, attorneys, insurance agent, personal assistant, and financial planner. In reviewing Bill's financial matters, the group discovers that his $20 million homeowner's policy has expired. Bill has no coverage for his home!

What do you think every single professional adviser in the room would say? There is no debate here. They would all agree: get the house insured—immediately. But does Bill need to insure his home? No. He is worth billions of dollars. If his house fell into the lake, he could certainly afford to rebuild it. So then, why would most professionals agree that Bill should, in fact, insure his house? The answer: There is no need—but there is value; it is the value of Bill's home that should be insured.

So then I ask: Does your life have value? Of course it does. How then should you calculate your life's value in determining the amount of insurance coverage you should be carrying? To answer this question, we have to move from the need amount to the *human life value* (HLV) method of calculation. Unless you base your coverage on the HLV model, you will continue to be grossly underinsured. Indeed, the reason many, perhaps most, Americans are vastly underinsured is that the HLV method of viewing insurance is so commonly overlooked.

To begin to understand how the HLV model works, let's take a difficult side journey back to the twin towers of the World Trade Center on September 11, 2001. Let's contemplate the horrible death and destruction wrought by the terrorists on that fateful day—and the economic losses suffered by the families whose loved ones perished. To address their economic losses, most life insurance agents might have looked simplistically at the amount of funds the surviving family members needed just to get by. But fortunately the attorneys and accountants who managed the 9/11 Victims' Compensation Fund astutely applied the HLV model—calculating the estimated future earnings of the deceased in each settlement.

So here is the headline: If you do not own at least $2.1 million in life insurance coverage, you are probably underinsured. And here is why this headline carries a powerful truth: The $2.1 million amount was the average amount the 9/11 Victims' Compensation Fund awarded to surviving family members. The *average* award for economic loss was $2.1 million. Mind you, these settlements, on average $2.1 million, were not awarded in consideration of pain and suffering or gross negligence—events for which juries commonly award large sums. No. These awards were based on the potential earning power of those deceased income earners.

The $2.1 million amount represents a simple truth about all of us who work for a living: the economic value of our lives is huge. The amount of money that each of us will earn in a lifetime—with raises, inflation, benefits, bonuses, promotions, profit sharing—is a multimillion-dollar sum. If you make $40,000 or $50,000 annually, your life's economic value may be about $2.1 million. If you make over $100,000 annually, your life's economic value is much greater.

> Headline: If you do not own at least $2.1 million in life insurance coverage, you are probably underinsured.

If you are currently working, do you have a number of years before you will retire? What is your life's economic value to your family? There are some sophisticated ways to measure this value, but to get you in the ballpark, multiply your current annual earnings times the number of years until your expected retirement.

Here are two examples:

- If you are age 40 and you make $60,000 a year and you plan to work until age 62, then the math works out to $60,000 x 22 = $1,320,000. Do you have that much coverage?

- If you are 35 and you make $175,000 a year and you plan to work until age 65, then the math works out to about $5,250,000 of economic value.

Now, you may be asking yourself: Do I have enough coverage? Unfortunately, I can't answer that for you. Although the value of a human being can never be replaced, the economic value of a human life can be compensated.

Generally speaking, at a minimum, you should consider carrying the amount needed to maintain your family's lifestyle should a breadwinner die. At a maximum, you might insure your life to its full economic value. Most people, once they are fully aware of the concepts of *need* and *human life value*, choose something in between those two dollar amounts.

Questions about coverage amounts should be addressed to the person most directly affected—the nonworking spouse. The central question to ask is: Should our life insurance policy barely cover the current lifestyle or the full economic value of the working spouse's life? If both spouses are working, the question should be modified to contemplate the couple's combined earning power.

I began this chapter with fairly harsh criticism of my fellow financial planning professionals—your advisers. In writing this chapter, I do not

You Are
Grossly
Underinsured

mean for you to fire these people. To the contrary, I hope that the information in this chapter leads you to have serious dialogue with your advisers—tackling difficult issues and taking a clear and honest look at your financial goals and your financial profile.

Most financial advisers I know personally are ethical and caring and truly want what is best for their clients. But advisers are only human, and thus subject to bias and fear. So as you meet with your advisers, help them to help you. If they are unable or unwilling to discuss life insurance, ask them to refer you to someone who will work with you on this important element of your financial future.

The questions that follow will help you to start the dialogue with your advisers. Once you have the numbers on paper, plan to recalculate them periodically because both your need amount and your human life value may change dramatically over time.

Questions to discuss with your financial advisers:

1. Can you help me establish a range of insurance that I may want to consider—from the amount that is needed to maintain a basic lifestyle to the full economic value lost in the event of my (or my spouse's) death?

2. What is that range?
   Basic need amount = _____.
   —or—
   Human life value amount = _____. (economic value)

3. What do you think of my starting estimates?
   The amount required to preserve my family's lifestyle is approximately _____.
   The human life value of my life is about _____.
   The human life value for my spouse is about

   _____.

4. Regarding insurability, it is important for us to discuss the following issues about my health, my spouse's health, and the health history of my family members, which may affect my eligibility for life insurance or may affect my rating by the insurance company:

   _____
   _____
   _____

5. Would you mind sharing with me how much life insurance you personally carry? Are you insuring your need amount, your human life value, or some amount in between?

2

Ten Myths About Life Insurance

In this chapter, I loosely use the word *myths* to convey the fictions, half-truths, misconceptions, and erroneous thinking that may have placed you and your dependents in financial jeopardy.

What follows is a listing of the ten myths about life and insurance and my ten brief, mostly tongue-in-cheek responses. The list is followed by some *serious* discussion of the issues, based on my professional insights and personal experiences.

The Ten Myths in Brief

1. *Financial industry professionals are just trying to sell you something.* Yes. You got me on that one. But now ask yourself, Why?

2. *It is best to pay the least for a policy.* Sure, just like you want to pay the least for a parachute before you make your first jump.

3. *You need life insurance only until the kids are out of the house.* Get real. The kids won't ever be out of the house.

4. *Life insurance is a rip-off.* The lottery is a rip-off. Life insurance is just a product.

5. *You could be worth more dead than alive.* This isn't the Wild, Wild West. Relax. It is impossible for any of us to be worth more dead than alive.

6. *It is a bad idea to mix investments and insurance.* I've found from experience that it is a bad idea to mix rum, beer and wine, but mixing investments and insurance is a very good idea, as you will learn by reading forward.

7. *The insurance policy with the highest illustrated values wins.* Illustrations—documents summarizing the terms of an insurance policy based on "typical" scenarios—are guaranteed to be wrong in reality. The best financial strategies win, not the most attractive illustrations.

8. *Term insurance is cheap.* And there's a reason it is cheap!

9. *Whole life is the only way to create a guaranteed death benefit.* It is one way, but not the only way.

10. *You are not going to die.* If you doubt this one, this book may not help you.

These myths, while possibly humorous, are dangerous. Potentially, they spell financial jeopardy for those you love. So let's examine these myths one by one. Once these are examined, you will be done mythologizing and will be in a much better position to make sound, rational decisions as you implement a life insurance strategy for your family.

Myth #1: Financial industry professionals are all just trying to sell you something.

This myth is true in part. Although I am not here to sell you anything, I do want you to "buy in" on some important ideas that affect the financial solvency of you and your family. I have no personal stake in whether you act on those ideas. The main idea I want you to buy in to is the idea of responsibility—your responsibility to make solid financial decisions for your family. Clearly, you deserve some credit here. You are feeling the tug of responsibility because you are studying the information this book offers.

So now you ask: What's the next step? Answer: Consult with **your** financial advisers. And go into every meeting knowing that most **financial** professionals do want to sell you something. They want to sell **you** on making solid decisions. If you find yourself not trusting your advis-ers—questioning either their integrity or their competence—then by all means find professionals whom you do trust. If you don't have a financial adviser, ask a trusted friend for a referral.

As you go into consultations with your advisers, be wary of this little secret, one that you may have already sensed: Many advisers will let you get away with buying far too little life insurance so long as you buy something. Ironic, don't you think? Insurance professionals—so often accused of "just trying to sell something"—are more likely to be underselling their products. I know this could be true about your agents because I have been there myself. In years past, I left many a consultation thinking to myself: These clients really should have more coverage than they chose, but at least I tried. I can't force them to do what is right. They're going to do what they're going to do.

Your advisers have the information, the answers, the details—the good, the bad, the ugly about the insurance products available. Ask them, and let them help you make the best decision possible. That best deci-

Term Insurance:	Provides a death benefit paid out for a specified term or period of time—such as 1 year, 10 years, 20 years, and so on. A term insurance policy does not build up any cash values. Having a term policy is like renting a home versus buying one.
Permanent Insurance:	Consists of both a term insurance element as well as a cash value accumulation. As the name implies, it is often intended to be used over the course of a lifetime until the time of death. Having permanent insurance is analogous to owning instead of renting a home throughout one's lifetime. Permanent insurance varies as follows:
Whole Life:	A policy that runs for the "whole life" of the insured. Premiums are usually paid for the "whole life" as well.
Universal Life:	Term plus a fixed interest rate, similar to a CD interest rate, paid by the insurance company.
Variable Universal Life:	Term plus a wide range of investment options, including a fixed account and related mutual fund-like subaccounts.

sion is going to be made with them and with their help, not by you alone.

What I am saying here is that you may have to exercise courage and take the lead as you go forward with your advisers. Signal to them that you want a candid dialogue about coverage amounts that factor in your life's economic value—not just the amounts needed to sustain a given standard of living. With all your information on the table, let the professionals instruct you on what kinds of coverage and how much coverage is appropriate for you—which leads us to the next myth.

Myth #2: It is best to pay the least for an insurance policy.

If it were always best to pay the least in life, then we would all be driving Kia compacts. Now, if you are a proud owner of the Kia brand, please take no offense and understand what I am saying here. We often buy based solely on price—but at other times we buy based on value. What do you value in a car? If you value safety more than any other feature, then perhaps you drive a Volvo. Or if you value high-end performance and handling, you may own a Porsche or a BMW. As with vehicles, if all that mattered was the price of a life insurance policy, then everyone would be best served owning the cheapest form—*term insurance* (as opposed to *permanent insurance*). Most people who purchase term insurance do so thinking: I pay the least, and if I die, the insurer pays through the nose. What's the big deal? Term insurance is just a commodity.

Anyone's Story

A man had a bothersome creak in his wood floor. He tried for months to remedy this aggravating noise. He tried nails. He tried wood glue. He tried ignoring it. He tried covering the creaky spot with a rug. All of his attempts were to no avail. Finally, begrudgingly, he hired a carpenter to fix the creak. The carpenter asked some questions. He walked up and down the floor assessing the creaky sounds. Then he reached into his tool belt and pulled out a 3/8-inch wood screw. He pulled out his electric screwdriver. He knelt down. In less than 10 seconds, he set the screw. He walked up and down the offending area three times to determine that the creaky sound was no more. Then he walked over to a table and wrote out his invoice:

Fixing the floor: $10

Knowing how to fix the floor: $100

Total: $110

Well, this thinking is true to a point—but only to a point. And this thinking may be fine for a few people—but is it right for you? Maybe you should buy term insurance from the cheapest source and without professional guidance if you can answer with complete confidence questions such as:

- Should I have 10-, 15-, 20-, or 30-year term insurance? Why? What happens at the end of the period?

- Should my spouse own the policy, or should I own it? Or should a trust own it?

- Is the term policy convertible? To what and under what circumstances?

- Who should be the primary and secondary beneficiaries of my policies?

- How will the insurance proceeds, paid to my children before they reach age 18, be managed?

> Don't pay the minimum on a permanent, variable universal life insurance policy. Pay the maximum.

In more than 20 years as a financial adviser, I have yet to encounter even one client who could formulate clear and confident answers to these questions (and those appearing at the end of this chapter) without considerable professional input. The insurance field is complex and dynamic—challenging even the professionals to stay abreast.

While we're on the subject of buying cheap, there's more. Not only should you be willing to pay a bit more for a term insurance policy that comes with all the important questions asked and answered (with the help of your advisers), but also you should pay, in many instances, the maximum for permanent insurance.

You read that right. When a *universal life* or *variable universal life* insurance policy allows for a range between a minimum premium and a maximum premium, pay the maximum you can without jeopardizing the tax advantages of the policy. The headline is: Don't pay the minimum on a permanent, variable universal life policy. Pay the maximum. (Chapter 4 will elaborate on this point.)

Why pay the maximum premium allowed? Well, think of how an airline works. Suppose that flying an aircraft with 250 seats from Los Angeles to New York takes 50 passengers just to break even. How many seats does the airline want to fill? Of course it wants to fill all 250 seats—the first 50 to cover the operating costs and the remaining 200 to make a profit—to be the most effective financially.

To carry the analogy to life insurance, if you have a minimally funded policy, you pay the cost and a bit more. In contrast, with a maximum-funded policy, you "fly your airplane full." That is, you pay your cost plus every dollar up to the maximum that the IRS allows. This approach allows you to pay your costs and to accumulate investment dollars efficiently and with powerful tax advantages.

A Buddha Story

A man stood before Buddha. Buddha said to him, "What can I do for you, my son?"

The man said, "Buddha, I have a problem."

Buddha said, "Of course you do. We all have problems."

"*Everyone* has problems?" the man asked.

Buddha answered, "Yes, in fact, everyone has 25 problems."

The man asked incredulously, "Does every person have 25 problems, Buddha?"

Buddha replied, "Well, not everyone. The man who does not know he has 25 problems has 26 problems."

So it is, as with any other important purchase, when you are contemplating a life insurance policy, consider both price and value—the price and value of the policy itself as well as the price and value of the financial advice that informs your decisions.

Myth #3: You need life insurance only until the kids are out of the house.

You know, don't you, that the kids never really leave. Sure, they may physically leave, but the connections grow deeper and more complex as time passes. The relationships broaden to include in-laws, grandchildren, and great-grandchildren. The freedoms we, as parents, envision when our children reach 18 or 21 years of age … well, those freedoms never really arrive. Instead, the timeline of connectivity extends and deepens and grows more complex.

> The need for life insurance doesn't go away; it just changes.

Myth #3 thinking goes something like this: When the kids are living on their own and the house mortgage is mostly paid down, I won't really need life insurance anymore. Admit it. Isn't that what you are thinking? Well, you are getting to know the routine by now. As in the wisdom of Buddha (see sidebar), when we solve one of the "25 challenges" in our lives, another crops up to replace it. So it is with life insurance. Just as the kids are leaving the nest, another purpose for protection arises.

Indeed, life insurance does not serve a single purpose for a fixed period of time, as we might wish. If, over the years leading up to retirement, we have done well accumulating wealth, the purpose of life insurance becomes one of estate planning. If we did not save enough for our own retirement because of costs associated with the kids' college educations, the purpose of life insurance becomes financial protection for our spouse in the later years of life. If our adult children are struggling financially as they support their young families, the purpose of life insurance might be financial protection for our grandchildren.

Reasons abound for why you might want to own life insurance throughout your life—and extending beyond to the lives of those you love. Term insurance is okay, but don't assume that there will be no need for insurance in the long run, only short term. Moreover, if you cannot afford "flying the plane full" with permanent life insurance, then purchase a *convertible term* policy. Later, when you do have the funds, you'll be able to convert some or all of your policy and thus keep it throughout your life.

Convertible Term Similar to regular term insurance, but with the privilege to convert the coverage to a permanent policy during the period of years the term insurance is in effect. This is an important distinction and should always be considered when purchasing a term policy.

In Chapter 3, we will consider the strategies for purchasing various types of life insurance and in the right amounts—in anticipation of life's milestones. But for now, the headline reads: The need for life insurance doesn't go away; it just changes.

Myth #4: Life insurance is a rip-off.

It is puzzling that so many people express hatred toward life insurance companies. The headline should read: Instead of ripping people off, insurance companies provide security for our families and peace of mind for us.

Life insurance is just like any other business. Each company competes with many others offering similar products. The companies couldn't rip you off if they wanted to. The competition would drive them out. This is how it works. Based on actuarial tables first developed by Edmond Haley (of Haley's Comet fame), insurance companies calculate the risk of a person dying at any given age. The companies then set their premiums according to those calculated risks. The premium you pay reflects those calculated (actuarial) risks. Therefore, all life insurance is term insurance—with different packaging according to consumer needs. (See definitions in the sidebars and in the Glossary. More on the distinctions will come in Chapter 5.) Beyond the term amount, the company adds a small amount more—the margin required to cover operating costs and to

Instead of ripping people off, insurance companies provide security for our families and peace of mind for ourselves.

earn a profit. (That's what businesses are supposed to do—make profits. After all, you want the insurance company to survive for when it is time for your policy's payout.)

What keeps the costs in check is competition, inherent in good old-fashioned capitalism—the same dynamics that drive pricing in any other industry. Yes, your insurance company will earn some profit, but not so much to preclude competitors from putting it out of business with far more favorable pricing.

In actuality, Myth #4 thinking is a smoke screen put up by people who find the entire life insurance decision-making process tedious. With mythical thinking, they make a case for avoiding the insurance topic altogether. Also, the smoke screens work to throw off financial advisers, who are easily discouraged from pressing the subject. Many advisers don't want to spar with their clients.

Nevertheless, your advisers should see your smoke screen for what it is: a call for help. And they should fulfill their professional obligations to you by educating you with the facts and then standing back to let you make fully informed decisions on your own behalf. Indeed, you *are* getting ripped off—if your financial advisers are letting you walk away from the table grossly underinsured without telling you the truth.

Myth #5: You could be worth more dead than alive.

This one is easy. It is impossible to be worth more dead than alive. The major headline is: It is impossible to be overinsured with life insurance. So just stop worrying about this one. It is never going to happen. You can't purchase too much life insurance even if you try. Here's why: If you were to apply for $20 million in coverage, the insurance company would turn you down—unless your future earning power warranted such a large amount.

You may ask: Aren't they just trying to sell more insurance? Wouldn't they be happy to sell me as much coverage as I am willing to buy? Answer: No. They will sell only up to, and not a penny more than, what you are worth financially. Another way of saying this is they will insure only up to, and no more than, your economic value—your human life value.

It is impossible to be overinsured with life insurance.

Never, in my 20 years as a financial adviser, has a new client walked into my office already insured for his or her full human life value. Too many to count have said: "I don't want to be overinsured," or "I don't want to be worth more dead than alive." Such comments simply show naiveté.

The irony is that most agents are dramatically underselling, not overselling, the amount of coverage for their clients. If the $2.1 million average awarded by the 9/11 Victims' Compensation Fund serves as a benchmark, then probably no financial adviser has every client insured adequately based on full economic human life value.

Myth #6: It is a bad idea to mix investments and insurance.

This is one of those mythical gems that if you repeat it often enough you can start to believe it. You know a headline must be coming, so here it is: It is *great* to mix investments and insurance. And with that one simple statement, I have thousands of financial services professionals who "believe" otherwise up in arms. I say, again, it is not about belief systems; it is about knowing and understanding tools, concepts, and strategies. When the right tool is used in conjunction with the right concept and strategy, mixing investments and insurance can be a powerful thing to behold.

One caveat, however, requires mention here: It is a great idea to create a mix of investments and insurance when "flying your plane full"—not when flying three-quarters empty. (See previous Myth #2.) In other words, mix— but mix the right insurance and investment products in the right proportions.

> Actually, it's *great* to mix investments and insurance.

Why is it not just good but great to mix investments and insurance? Simple. For the tax savings. Using one approach, you can invest in taxable instruments, such as mutual funds or certificates of deposit (CDs). With this approach you pay tax on your earnings while paying for term insurance with after-tax dollars. Alternatively, you can invest in tax-deferred (eventually tax-free) accounts, including money market funds as well as stock and bond accounts. With this approach, you pay for the term insurance with pretax dollars. Using this latter approach, you benefit from tax-advantaged investing and pretax insurance costs.

In my professional practice, I encourage clients to implement both approaches in a deliberate strategy to diversify investment dollars into the three financial plan "buckets" available to us all: (1) taxable investments, (2) tax-deferred investments, and (3) tax-free investments. Without the third bucket funded adequately, all income at retirement becomes entirely taxable. (You will find more detailed discussion on this subject in Chapter 4.)

To repeat, without the third bucket funded properly, all of your income at the time of your retirement will be fully taxable. So set aside your Myth #6 thinking and go mix! Combine the tax advantages of insurance with the investment flexibility of mutual funds—while paying for your insurance costs with pretax dollars.

Myth #7: The insurance policy with the highest illustrated values wins.

The term *illustration* in the insurance context refers to the scenarios prepared by the insurance companies to assist financial advisers in counseling clients about insurance products. The illustrations include information such as sales charges, surrender charges (should you cash out in the early years of the policy), cash values, and exclusions. Insurance commissioners require clients to sign these illustrations as evidence of full disclosure.

> It's not the illustration that matters—but the quality of the financial advice. To wit, it's the adviser that matters.

The problem with illustrations is that clients tend to interpret them as promises when in fact they are based solely on sets of hypothetical conditions. This situation calls for a headline: It's not the illustration that matters—but the quality of the financial advice. To wit, it's the adviser that matters.

Admittedly, illustrations do show guaranteed features of the policy—but the illustrations are mostly a constructed bunch of assumptions that are not going to be true over a long period of time. (For example, how can anyone accurately predict earnings on the cash values of an insurance policy 30 or 40 years into the future? No company has a crystal ball that clear.)

Nonetheless, the insurance industry is competing furiously with such illustrations. Accountants like to use illustrations to decide which policy is best. But illustrations are fraught with fine print and far-reaching assumptions. Worse yet, we financial advisers have great difficulty understanding how to compare the illustrations—although we battle each other all day long over competing illustrations. In the balance are our clients who have no chance of interpreting the complexities and implications that underlie the illustrated numbers.

Reviewing life insurance illustrations can be something like venturing down the rabbit hole in *Alice in Wonderland*. In that scene, Alice enters a world where nothing is normal; nothing is as it seems. Characters talk in strange riddles, things look bigger or smaller than they should be, and the white knight walks backward. It is weird and confusing—just like an insurance illustration. When, after 20 or 30 minutes of reviewing the illustrations, you emerge from this strange trip, you (and your advisers) are more confused than when you entered.

My point is that insurance illustrations should never begin the dialogue between advisers and clients. Instead, financial counseling should start with considering the financial goals or the financial problems that need solving. Advisers should set forth alternative strategies and offer the gamut of products available. Only after these considerations should the client choose among the many product options. And only after the client has chosen a product should advisers review the relevant illustration as a means of complete disclosure. Unfortunately, most advisers circumvent background exploration of the financial objectives and product alternatives. Instead, they go directly to the illustration—selling the client on one product with the claim "My product is better than their product."

In reality, most reputable insurance companies have competitive products. Clients will be well served with most solid companies and their insurance products. So the more important question becomes not which insurance company and product to choose—but what financial strategy best meets the stated financial objective or need. Determining the best strategy leads to choosing the right products. Some policies are better suited for smokers, some for estate planning purposes, some for the seriously ill, and so forth.

Consequently, the financial advice—more than the product choice—is paramount. Choosing the product is secondary to developing the best financial strategy to meet a stated financial objective. If you are making decisions based on which illustration looks better, you are caught up in a nasty game. So please leave Myth #7 thinking behind in the knowledge that life insurance illustrations guarantee only one thing—black ink sticks to white paper!

Myth #8: Term insurance is cheap.

Alas, this one, too, must go to make way for a new headline: Term insurance is cheap because insurers rarely pay out for it. Actually, term insurance is *not* cheap—at least not in the sense that you are probably thinking. What I call "pure" term insurance—the kind without any cash value associated with it—at first glance is less costly than permanent insurance. But cheap? Let's take a closer look.

First, let's explore whether term insurance is a good value. Out of every 100 policies, 99 of them never pay out. That seems like more of a good deal for the insurers than for the 99 policyholders who paid premiums for years yet never collected a cent. You ask, How does this happen? Answer: 99% of the policyholders dropped their policies long before their deaths. Out of 100 policyholders, only one died while still holding coverage. You ask again, How

> Term insurance is cheap because insurers rarely pay out for it.

does this happen? Answer: It happens because of Myth #3 thinking that says we need life insurance only while the kids are still at home. Instead of carrying coverage until death, most policyholders, by design, choose to carry it only during the years that they are unlikely to die—during their 30s, 40s, 50s, or 60s. With average life expectancy in the late 70s or even into the 80s, such people are left with no life insurance coverage at the time when they are actually likely to die.

Don't get me wrong. Term insurance is a great fit, perhaps the only fit, for families needing a lot of death benefit but with very limited funds. But as soon as my clients have money available to fund a permanent policy, I counsel them to convert some of the term. I want them to own life insurance when they are actually going to use it. With term, there is only a 1% chance their beneficiaries will ever collect.[2]

"Pure" term insurance costs the consumer 43 cents more on every dollar compared with permanent insurance purchased with tax-deferred dollars.

Next, let's examine another element of the "term is cheap" myth. If you compare the pricing of the term insurance component embedded within a permanent policy versus a "pure" term insurance policy, the cost per each thousand dollars of coverage is cheaper for the pure term policy. But a closer look reveals that the pure term policy is paid with after-tax dollars. For example, an insurance consumer with earnings in a 30% tax bracket has to earn $1.43 to have one dollar left (after tax) to buy one dollar's worth of term insurance. Contrast that to the term component within a permanent insurance policy purchased with tax-deferred dollars. In this scenario, each dollar buys one dollar of coverage. So the headline reads: "Pure" term insurance (the kind that pays out only 1% of the time) costs the consumer 43 cents more on every dollar compared with permanent insurance purchased with tax-deferred dollars.

If you still want to hang on to Myth #8, consider yet one more fact. If, in the future, a pure term policyholder were to decide to keep the coverage beyond the term of the policy, the costs would skyrocket. Typically, extending a 20-year term beyond the 20th year—get ready for a shocker—increases costs by many factors. The example in the sidebar table shows you the math. Take my word for it. You are not likely to want term insurance past the term—unless you have one foot in the grave.

As you can see, the jump—from $1,450 a year in the first 20 years to $31,140 in the 21st year, and higher in each subsequent year—is so prohibitively expensive that almost everyone drops their term insur-

---

2 Dr. Arthur Williams, "Some Empirical Observations on Term Life Insurance: Revisited" University of Pennsylvania, 1980.

ance policies before they die. Would you want to pay $375,700 for one year of coverage?

Cost Example: Term Life Insurance

The following example shows the cost (premiums) paid over the life (term) of a $1 million term life insurance policy purchased by a client with a *preferred rating*—a nonsmoker at age 41.

Year of Term	Premiums per Year	Comment
1st–20th	$ 1,450	
21st	$ 31,140	
22nd	$ 34,500	
23rd	$ 38,300	
24th	$ 42,550	
30th	$ 77,900	
35th	$ 131,120	
40th	$ 214,430	< The client is now 81—the life expectancy of most Americans.
45th	$ 375,700	

If you are "connecting the dots," you may have realized that since all insurance is term insurance, the costs in the permanent policies, too, must be going up as policyholders age. Yes, absolutely. All life insurance is term insurance, and insurance premiums are more expensive for older consumers. Nevertheless, permanent insurance policyholders who have been paying more than the minimum over years have accumulated additional, tax-deferred cash—making the policy affordable even at ages 70, 80, 90, and 100 years.

So you see, dispelling Myths #2 and #8 along with "flying the plane full" can reap all kinds of benefits over the course of however many decades of life you have remaining.

Myth #9: Whole life is the only way to create a guaranteed death benefit.

If having the guarantee of a death benefit—no matter what happens with interest rates or with the stock market—is of grave (pun intended) importance to you, you have several good options. Let's briefly review them.

You can secure a guaranteed death benefit, no matter what happens, with a whole life policy. For many years, this product has been the one of choice for those seeking death benefit guarantees. But additional options are now available for consideration.

Whole Life A form of term insurance that runs for the insured's "whole life." The policyholder usually pays the premiums for his or her "whole life." Whole life comes with the guarantee that if the required payments are made as scheduled, the death benefits are guaranteed.

Fixed Universal Life The same as universal life. These policies have a combination of term insurance and a cash accumulation account. A fixed universal account pays interest at current market rates, similar to certificate of deposit (CD) or money market rates.

Death Benefit Guarantee Universal Life Similar to universal life but with death benefit guarantees, as in whole life policies. The policyholder receives the guarantees of a whole life policy, but with greater flexibility in how the premiums are paid.

As an alternative to whole life, you can secure a guaranteed death benefit with a *fixed universal life* policy. Compared with whole life, fixed universal policies have a bit more flexibility. They may provide the same death benefit guarantees, but they offer policyholders more control—especially in the manner that premiums are paid and when.

Another option—one fairly new to the industry—is *death benefit guarantee universal life*. This option combines some of the best elements of universal life and whole life insurance policies. Often the cost to obtain the guarantees is less than the cost of a comparable whole life policy.

Finally, you can secure death benefit guarantees with a variable universal life policy. Be wary of agents who try to scare you with tales of dramatic stock market losses and policies that never pay out. If you are seeking death benefit guarantees, you can pay a premium similar to whole life, embedded into a variable policy. That way, no matter how the stock market performs, your death benefit is guaranteed. And if you "fly your plane full" by paying the maximum premium the IRS allows, you automatically get the death benefit guarantee.

Thus, the new headline reads: Whole life, death benefit guarantee universal life, fixed universal life, and variable universal life are simply financial tools. Some tools work better than others in some situations. They are all worth consideration.

Myth #10: You are not going to die.

For this discussion, we will set aside any ponderings about the possibilities of reincarnation. What is germane in this context is that someday your physical body will give out.

Of course you don't really believe that you are never going to die—you just act as if you believe it. At least you have acted as if you believe

---

Whole life, fixed universal life, and variable universal life are simply financial tools. Some work better than others in some situations.

---

in your immortality up until now—until seriously focusing on the financial jeopardy that you have placed yourself and your family in by being grossly underinsured.

Closely related to belief in Myth #10 is the I'm-not-going-to-die-until-I'm-very-old corollary. Clinging to this idea, you figure that you will have accumulated plenty of money by the end of your life so that there is no need to buy life insurance. You may be right, and you may be wrong. I don't know. I do know the odds, though—thanks again to Edmond Haley's actuarial tables. The likelihood that you will live beyond your life expectancy is 50%. Great! So if you do a good job of saving and investing throughout your long life—and if you become financially independent by the end, perhaps you have no traditional need for life insurance. But there is a 50% chance that you will die before your life expectancy.

50-50. Them's the odds. Yes, for each one of us—doctor lawyer, Indian chief, or chief bottle washer—same odds. We're all in the 50-50 lotto.

How do you think the actuaries (like Mr. Haley) predict the date of our death? They draw a line between the half of us who will die early and the half of us who will die later. The demarcation line is the expected date of death. Each of us has a 50-50 chance of falling to either side of the line. Which brings us to the most major headline of all: There is a 50% likelihood that you will die before your life expectancy.

> There is a 50% likelihood that you will die before your life expectancy.

Thus, I implore you, dear reader: Get adequately insured—just in case you wind up on the wrong side of that 50-yard line (to mix a metaphor). And while you are at it, be sure to adequately insure, if applicable, the stay-at-home spouse of your family. (Chapter 6 will address the reasons your spouse needs coverage—in ways more critical than what you might assume.)

In closing, let's review the odds in Myth #10: 100% and 50%. Can you assign each percentage to the appropriate concept? Yes, 50% of us will live beyond our life expectancy, and 50% of us will die before our life expectancy. And finally, 100% of us will die some day.

So goes the somewhat humorous and completely treacherous ten myths of life insurance. Maybe they have been fun for you—but now the smoke is lifting from your smoke screens, and you are just beginning to see more clearly. The chapters that follow will explore in greater depth the alternatives to your previous mythical thinking. But first, we'll run through a list of questions you now have for discussion with your trusted advisers.

Questions to discuss with your financial advisers:

1. What is the long-term strategy for my life insurance? Does it serve just one purpose or are there multiple purposes that may be served over time?

2. How much term and how much permanent insurance should I have? Why?

3. Should I have a 10-, 15-, 20-, or 30-year term? Why?

4. Should I own the policy? Should my wife? Should a trust? What are the implications of each type of ownership?

5. Who should be the primary beneficiary—who should be the secondary beneficiary—of my policies?

6. What happens if my children are eligible to receive the payout before they are 18? How do we avoid court intervention? Who will handle any large sums of money on their behalf?

7. Is the term policy convertible? To what? Under what circumstances? When, or why, might I want to convert the term policy?

8. How am I paying for my life insurance now—pretax or after-tax? Why?

9. Should I increase or decrease my coverage next year and in following years? With my current permanent insurance, am I "flying the plane full"? Why or why not? Please show me a *reprojection* (sometimes called an *in-force ledger*) on my current policy to see how it is likely to perform in the coming years at the current premium level.

10. What percentage of my assets is currently in taxable accounts, tax-deferred accounts, and tax-free accounts? How can my life insurance complement the financial strategy of building more money in the tax-free "bucket"?

11. What are the advantages and disadvantages of purchasing group term insurance through my employer?

12. What is going on with the insurance company I am going to use? Will it be here to pay the claim should I die? How can I know this?

Reprojection Also referred to as an in-force ledger, a reprojection is an update of a policy that is in force. Using current values and projections, the reprojection demonstrates whether the policy, as designed, will perform to the client's expectations over time. It can be used to guide discussions about funding levels, the amount of the premium to pay, and other aspects of policy management.

3

Time Diversification

If we could predict the future, we would never need to diversify. If we knew which stock or mutual fund would be the top performer over the next year, why would we buy any other investment!

So it goes with time. If we knew in advance about such things as when we would die, whether we would suffer a disability, whether we would need long-term care at some point—if we could predict these events in advance, then we could take appropriate steps to deal with them before their arrival.

But you don't know your future—nor do I. And so we need not only to diversify instruments of our investments, we need to diversify them over time—across the various stages of life. In this chapter, as you read about time diversification, picture your life along this timeline:

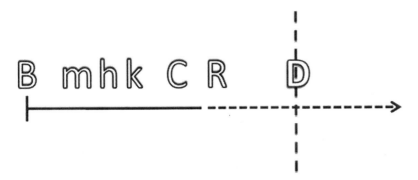

Because this book is addressed primarily to families, the timeline is based on certain assumptions. In this example, the capital *B* represents the date you were born. The *m* stands for the day you marry. You buy a home (*h*), have kids (*k*), and the kids go to college (a capital *C*—the capital representing the level of financial pain associated with this event). Eventually, you want to have financial independence and the ability to retire (*R*). And finally, capital *D*. Guess what the D stands for? Yup, right you are.

Notice where D is placed on the timeline and the sliding scale to either side. The eventuality of your death can move dramatically in one direction or the other. In this example, I put D out around the time in life when the actuaries predict we all will die. But of course no one dies on this predicted date. Actually, 50% of us will live beyond the predicted date, and 50% of us will die before. The fact is that we don't know—nor do the actuaries. We don't know whether we will live to the right side of the actuarial date, outlasting our life expectancy—or die "early," at some point to the left of the actuarial prediction.

In fact, the entire timeline is iffy. The dates for all the events can slide around on the scale. Other events not shown pop up along the way that can affect us financially: kids' weddings, divorces, second homes, business start-ups, new roofs, car purchases. Maybe a financial setback delays our desired retirement date.

So the timelines of our lives have many unknowns. This unpredictability is part of the fun and the mystery of living. Knowing too much about the future is the stuff of *Twilight Zone* and scary movies. We are not meant to know the future, so uncertainty leaves us with some important decisions in the game of life.

Some people play the life game like a Las Vegas roulette wheel, placing bets in hopes of "beating the house." They bet on not needing life insurance before they have accumulated enough money to gain financial independence. They bet on making it to retirement without suffering a long-term disability. They bet on making enough money to retire someday.

But most of us don't want to bet against the odds on such outcomes that spell the difference between financial solvency and financial disaster. There is just too much at stake for our families. There are too many unknowns that defy prediction—questions like: Will we have enough to live on 20 years beyond our life expectancy? Will we become physically or mentally disabled at some point, and if so for how long? Will we need long-term care in our retirement years—or worse, will we be among the 37% who need long-term care before the age of 60? Will we die well beyond our life expectancy, or close to it, or long before?

The central answer to all of these unknowns is that we should diversify our financial strategies throughout our lifetimes. Most people, however, view their need for life insurance within the upward-pointing arrows on this timeline:

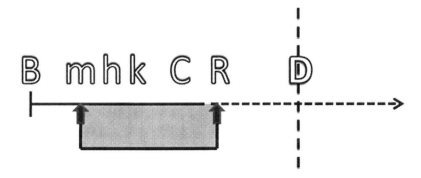

People think it appropriate to have life insurance coverage starting around the time they marry and up to the time they retire. Seems logical. This scenario may actually be the case—for a few. But most of us will have a multitude of reasons to own life insurance from a very young age (just after birth in some cases) to beyond our deaths. Some of these reasons are not apparent to you. Some show up at later stages along the timeline. We'll explore a number of these not-so-obvious reasons to own insurance from age 1 to age 101.

Let's start at age 1. You may ask: Why on earth would anyone ever want to own insurance on the life of a one-year-old? Answer: Owning life insurance on children can create money in the event they die young. This notion may seem macabre to you. But for a family of very modest means, life insurance could take care of funeral costs. Of course such a family should first insure both parents adequately.

Here are several additional reasons to consider insuring the life of a young child:

- To protect the child's insurability when the possibility of genetically linked disease exists

- To save toward a college education

- To control taxes

Let's explore each of these reasons in some detail.

If a family's genetics include certain inheritable diseases, it may make sense to purchase life insurance while the children are young and still insurable. If, for example, a child at age 13 is diagnosed with juvenile diabetes, insurers may deny applications for life insurance, thereby posing a great financial burden to the family. Such situations are increasingly likely as scientists identify genetic links to many diseases and as more insurance companies require genetic testing as part of the underwriting process. In the future, insurance may not be available to applicants who are genetically predisposed to certain illnesses.

Mark's Story

My friend Scott, a manager in an office of financial advisers, found out a couple of years ago that his teenage son, Mark, has juvenile diabetes. While it is likely that Mark will finish college, get married, and raise a family, he will find it expensive, or even impossible, to purchase life insurance due to his illness. If a $1 million life insurance policy had been purchased shortly after Mark's birth (and long before this illness showed up), Mark's future family would have the protections of life insurance coverage. Instead, Mark may come to depend heavily on group term insurance through his future employers. Also, he may find himself making many of his career decisions based on insurance benefits offered by employers rather than following his own heart's desires and dreams.

In addition, the rising costs of college tuition provide reason to insure the lives of young children. With the advent of the tax-favored 529 college savings plans, this strategy has lost some of its luster. Parents like the tax advantages of a 529 plan, but some parents don't like the "handcuffs" of that plan. A 529 plan has the advantage of tax-free growth and tax-free withdrawals, but the revenues generated must be used only for educational expenses. An alternative strategy might be a fully funded, variable universal life policy—especially if there is at least 15 years to contribute to the policy and to allow for tax-deferred compounding to grow the invested dollars.

Lastly, tax incentives provide perhaps the most compelling reason to insure a young child. Life insurance provides a tax-sheltered way to build a fortune that the IRS cannot touch. Imagine building tax-free dollars by using an extra three or four decades of compounding. Imagine how much tax-deferred money you could accumulate between age 1 and age 65 or 70—money that the IRS can't touch. The IRS can't touch the income that is taken tax-free—first through return of principal and later through tax-free and zero-cost loans. Moreover, the IRS can't touch the money when the remainder passes income tax-free to your child's eventual heirs (your future grandchildren, most likely). The IRS never sees a penny of the earnings or a penny of the insurance received by the heirs. We'll explore these investment concepts further in the next chapter.

Investing early in life can generate millions of dollars to be used later as tax-free, supplemental retirement income. The power is in tax-advantaged compounding, which really adds up the earlier in life one starts saving—as illustrated in the sidebar (*Your Story?*) example.

Your Story?

Your newborn child, upon reaching age 65, could accumulate $1.5 million to $2 million in wealth. Here's how. You invest just $100 a month starting upon her birth and continuing until she reaches young adulthood. Then as she begins working and earning, she continues to invest the same monthly amount in a variable universal life insurance policy until she reaches age 65. With roughly a 9% gross return on the $78,000 invested over the 65 years, your child will have accumulated $1.5 million or more. At age 65, she could start withdrawing $78,000 a year, every year (the same amount as the premiums invested) as tax-free, supplemental retirement income. And the IRS will have never seen a penny on any of the interest or capital gains generated with this policy.

Skeptics may say, "Yeah, but $1.5 million won't be worth that much 65 years from now." But any way you cut it, one and a half million is a lot of money. Plus, it will be $1.5 million more than if you never saved at all.

Those are some reasons for insuring young children. But what about insuring older offspring—at 15 or 20 years of age, for example? At any age, protecting against noninsurability and tax control may be desirable for parents—and for grandparents as well. Grandparents who have extra funds might invest in variable universal life insurance for their grandchildren to help them accumulate money toward the down payment on a home or toward the costs for a business start-up. Typically, in these scenarios, the grandparents own the policy and give it to the grandchildren when they reach maturity (as defined by the grandparents).

What about life insurance for adults further down the timeline—those married and with families? The need for insurance at this stage in life is obvious to most. The majority of adults want to provide for their survivors in the event of premature death—and that's 50% of us. Life insurance can pay off the mortgage and other debts, provide fully funded college educations, and ensure a reasonable lifestyle. Moreover, a policy based on the economic human life value of the deceased can provide much more than the basic financial needs of surviving family members (as described in Chapter 1).

Here are some other reasons for you to own life insurance in your 20s, 30s, 40s, and into your 50s:

- To provide for a handicapped child or family member

- To replace the income in the event of an untimely death of a working spouse

- To ensure continued tithing to your church

- To create a legacy for your family

- To create a legacy for your charitable wishes

- To diversify invested dollars for tax control (for more income later with less taxation)

- To provide liquidity for a business you own

Moreover, you may want life insurance, based on your human life value, in anticipation of the hundreds of other unpredicted reasons that may reveal themselves throughout your adult life.

Steve and Robin's Story

Steve and Robin, both age 39, met with their financial adviser, Elizabeth, to review their IRA and 401(k) accounts. At the time, Steve earned $130,000 annually servicing Fortune 100 accounts for a computer software firm. Robin earned about $90,000 annually as a pharmaceutical sales representative. Their three children ranged from 8 to 14 years of age.

After reviewing Steve and Robin's portfolio, Elizabeth offered appropriate advice about their diversification and about their life insurance coverage. Elizabeth concluded that the couple was drastically underinsured. Steve had $100,000 of group term coverage through his employer and a 20-year term policy worth $200,000 that he had purchased when the couple's first child was born. Robin had only one times her salary ($90,000) in group term through her employer.

After a few calculations, Elizabeth concluded that simply to maintain the family's current standard of living if either working spouse were to die, Steve would need an additional $750,000 of coverage and Robin would need at least $500,000. They went on to discuss the couple's potential lost income in the event of their deaths—their human life value (HLV) based on their projected future earnings. Steve's HLV was estimated to be at least $3 million and Robin's $2.1 million. As they talked, Elizabeth created the following table on the blackboard:

	Need	Human Life Value	Your Decision?
Steve	$ 750,000	$ 3,000,000	
Robin	$ 500,000	$ 2,100,000	

Thoughtfully, Steve and Robin agreed to purchase $2 million on Steve and $1.5 million on Robin in a combination of term and permanent life insurance policies.

Sadly, two years later, Robin lost her battle with ovarian cancer. Of course the family was devastated with the loss of a wife and mother of three. But as a result of the insurance proceeds ($90,000 from Robin's group policy and $1.5 million from the coverage purchased just two years before), the family was able to stay in their home and fund the college savings accounts for all three children. Steve could afford to take several months off work to spend time with the children and to mourn his loss. Upon returning to work, Steve took a slight pay cut in return for fewer trips and a better work schedule, enabling him to spend more time at home with his kids. In addition, Steve could afford a full-time nanny at $45,000 a year plus medical benefits, a car, and a retirement plan.

Although Robin's death had a tragic impact on their lives, Steve and his kids were able to mitigate their emotional loss because of the sound financial decisions that Robin and he had made two years earlier.

As you move further along the timeline—to about age 60—you probably reach a point when the kids are independent and doing well financially. Retirement for you is just around the corner. You are funded properly for a comfortable lifestyle in retirement. You are thinking that if you die or your spouse dies—no problem: The kids are squared away; the survivor will simply retire. You are thinking, Finally, no need for life insurance! Right? Answer: Maybe. It depends.

If the comfortable lifestyle you have planned is dependent on income streams derived from both spouses, the death of one could be problematic. Pensions may be lost or reduced. One of the social security income streams is lost. Big problem.

The fact is that like millions of American families, your family needs basic life insurance coverage, even in retirement. The surviving spouse will need insurance to maintain a desired lifestyle—what I call the "hidden need" for life insurance in retirement. Most financial advisers are so biased against life insurance for clients who are beyond retirement age that they forget to run the numbers on whether a basic need exists.

Conversely, what if your retirement is not shaky but is on a solid footing? What if you have plenty of income, no matter what happens to either spouse? In your case, you likely need to plan for estate liquidity. The larger your estate, the larger your need for immediate, liquid, tax-free dollars after death—especially the death of the second spouse.

We'll examine further the strategies associated with estate liquidity in Chapter 7.

For now, here is a partial list of reasons for you to own life insurance in your 60s and 70s:

- To supplement insufficient retirement cash flows

- To plan for estate liquidity—as one or both spouses die

- To equalize the estate so that the trusts established are properly funded

- To provide funds for family members in times of financial hardship

- To provide funds for a handicapped child or grandchild

- To control and diversify taxes

- To provide funds for the surviving spouse to pay the taxes on a Roth conversion of a large 401(k) or IRA

- To make all parties "whole" in the case of second marriages in which children from both marriages are heirs

- To allow for pension maximization (a strategy that allows you to take the highest pension payout and use life insurance to replace the pension should you die)

Beyond your 60s and 70s, the years pass—moving you yet further along the timeline. You are now at or beyond normal life expectancy. You may be thinking, Surely there is no reason to have life insurance at 80 or 90 years of age and beyond. To you, I answer, Your thinking is wrong.

In my opinion, the best people to insure are seniors 80 years of age and older. These folks know they are going to die. They appreciate that the insurance companies still regard them as having a human life value—in contrast to "society" that has written them off in more ways than one. They see the logic and wisdom in using the leverage and the tax advantages of life insurance in the later stages of life.

Still, you are probably thinking that it must be ridiculously expensive to insure an 80-year-old! Here, too, the IRS helps you in a couple of ways. First, the IRS requires very little death benefit for any lump sums invested at older ages. This means you can "fly the plane full"—and at your advanced age, you don't need a very big plane. To say it another way, the IRS permits us the tax-advantaged airplane—with a very small amount of life insurance required at older ages. So you can get the policy off the ground and fly to your destination quite nicely. Second, the money you have accumulated (and are probably not spending at age 80) is either creating unneeded taxable income every year, or it is growing tax-deferred and will be taxable to your heirs.

Alternatively, if at age 80 or older you can put a lump sum (large or small) into a life insurance policy, you will create tax-deferred growth for yourself and tax-free inheritances for your heirs. This approach is a capital transfer technique. You transfer taxable, nonleveraged dollars in exchange for tax-advantaged, leveraged dollars inside a life insurance policy.

Here are some additional reasons that you at age 80 or 90 might choose to have life insurance:

- To increase the legacy you leave to your family

- To create an additional legacy for your church or favorite charity—without reducing the inheritance you provide to your family

- To minimize taxes for yourself and your family

- To provide special funds for a unique family situation

- To receive gratification in the knowledge that, despite your advanced age, you are still insurable—and thereby still "worthwhile"

Bill and Hazel's story (sidebar) illustrates the use of life insurance by older folks. This story was provided to me by Jim McCarty, one of the best advisers out there helping his clients through creative applications with life insurance. I share this story with you because it provides a beautiful example of time diversification as a financial planning strategy. As this story demonstrates, life insurance can be used as a tool throughout our lives—and beyond.

Bill and Hazel's Story

My friend Jim was asked to join another adviser on a Saturday appointment with clients Bill and Hazel. Jim did not know a lot about the clients other than that they were both in their 80s and that they had $2 million in a single stock as well as some smaller amounts of cash and mutual funds.

After introductions, Jim asked, "Are you taking any of the dividends from your stock?" They answered that they were not.

"Are you then just letting the dividends accumulate on top of the existing principal?" Jim asked. They replied that that was their understanding.

"Do you anticipate needing any of this money for any reason—now or in the future?" Jim asked.

"No," Bill and Hazel answered in unison.

Then Jim asked, "Who will inherit your money when you both pass on?"

Bill responded, "My brother."

Jim gently pressed on. "Do you plan to leave anything to your children?" To this question, Hazel burst into tears.

Feeling mortified, Jim said, "I'm so sorry. Did I ask something too sensitive?"

Bill said, "Don't worry. It's just that we were never able to have children." Bill went on to explain that Hazel and he had always loved kids and loved spending time with them. For many years now, a group of young students had stopped by their home every afternoon after school for cookies and milk. In fact, Bill and Hazel planned their daily schedules so that they were always home in time "for the kids."

Jim looked intently at Bill and Hazel. "Please allow me to share a vision that came to me as you were talking. I see a beautiful park about the size of a whole block in this neighborhood. I see green, rolling hills of freshly mowed grass. There's a winding sidewalk with mothers pushing baby carriages and kids on bikes and skateboards. Over to one side is an area with slides and swings and a merry-go-round. Kids are laughing and screaming in mock terror as the spinning merry-go-round speeds up. I see a picnic area with grills and tables and places where adults in the community carry on your tradition—serving after-school snacks to kids. At the entrance is a large stone gateway with a black iron trellis arching over it. Flowers adorn the entrance, and ivy winds up and across the arch. If people stop for a moment as they pass through, they see a tasteful plaque—one that bears your names, the donors who made this wonderful scene possible—and the words *For the Kids*.

When Jim had finished describing his vision, he asked, "Can you, too, see the park clearly? If you could leave the $2 million of stock to Bill's brother and still manifest this legacy to your lives, would you be interested? The way is simple. You can leave the stock to your brother and at the same time allocate the dividends on that stock to a life insurance policy in your names—the proceeds for which will fund your park. Your brother gets his full inheritance—and the kids get their park."

If you are 30 years old, are you thinking at this stage of leaving money to build your life's legacy? Probably not. But there are a thousand other unforeseen financial challenges that you will face along the timeline of your life—challenges to which life insurance can provide opportunities.

As we see in Bill and Hazel's example, life insurance benefits can resonate powerfully and positively for many, many years after you are gone. But you don't have to die to benefit from life insurance. In the next chapter, we'll look at how you can save taxes—now and forever—using life insurance as the tool. And we'll look at how you can get your money back during your lifetime—without paying any taxes.

But before moving on, we'll review some additional questions you now have for your financial adviser concerning time diversification.

Questions to discuss with your financial advisers:

1. Should we consider insuring the kids?

2. If yes, how much coverage? Why? What type of insurance? Why?

3. How much coverage is needed simply to protect our family's current lifestyle if either spouse dies?

4. Should we use term or permanent or a combination of both? Why?

5. How does our current strategy provide us with flexibility, as we grow older?

6. Should we be discussing life insurance for our parents? Grandparents?

4

Tax Diversification

"I'm proud to be paying taxes in the United States. The only thing is—I could be just as proud for half the money."

Arthur Godfrey

Most investors find the concept of investment diversification easy to understand. Because we can never predict the "perfect investment" for the years ahead, we mitigate our risks by diversifying our investment portfolios. If we knew in advance what stock or fund would perform the best, we would never need to diversify. But most of us have been hurt financially whenever we have failed to diversify our investments. Anyone who was heavily invested in technology stocks when the "tech bubble" burst in the late 1990s can testify to the need for investment diversification.

In the previous chapter, we explored the importance of *time diversification*. Diversifying around the time dimension makes good sense—because we do not know with certainty whether our life spans will be shorter or longer than the actuarial tables predict or whether we will require long-term care at some stage in life. In the same vein, because we do not know what will happen with tax laws, tax rates, or tax brackets, we should diversify our investments around the tax dimension.

Although we cannot know the future—including the future of tax laws, tax rates, estate taxes—we can imagine possible scenarios stemming from today's realities, such as the "horror story" told in the sidebar. Can this future scenario happen? Certainly. Will it? We don't know, and that is the point. And when we don't know, it is good practice to consider diversification.

A Horror Story: A Glimpse into the Future

The year is 2026. Baby boomers have been retiring in droves for nearly 20 years. The strain on the social security system has been too much. The system simply cannot pay benefits as promised. Worse, the Medicare system is failing—at the very time when tens of millions of aged boomers are getting sick. The Medicare prescription plan signed into law by George W. Bush in 2005 is bankrupt. The only solution to the situation has been to cut benefits *and* to increase taxes. Average workers now pay over 30% of their weekly wages to the Social Security Administration—a measure implemented just to prevent the system from crumbling. Moreover, federal income tax rates have climbed to 45% for annual incomes over $50,000. Similarly, state income tax rates have also risen dramatically.

The problem, simply stated, is that too many boomers have strained federal and state resources. Something had to give, and it has—fewer benefits for increased taxes. But those who implemented prudent tax-diversification strategies many years back have realized enormous advantages through their tax-advantaged (especially tax-free) investment instruments.

Despite what is good common sense, most investors do not diversify around the tax dimension. (And few accountants even bring up the topic.)

The concept of tax diversification is fairly simple. Each dollar invested can be divvied among three types of accounts:

- Taxable

- Tax-deferred

- Tax-free

An even distribution across the three account types would be like three buckets of roughly equal proportions, as shown in Figure 1:

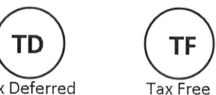

Taxable   Tax Deferred   Tax Free

Typical of most investors, however, the tax-free bucket is very skimpy—as illustrated in Figure 2:

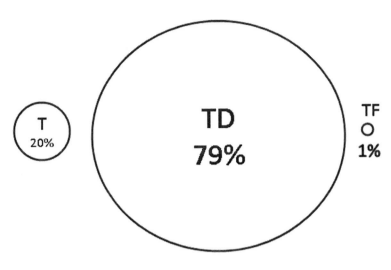

For ideal tax diversification, I recommend to my clients a mix represented by the buckets in Figure 3:

In the remainder of this chapter, you will discover my rationale for this investment mix based on the fact that each dollar invested has to go somewhere—and one of the ways to accumulate wealth is to use tax-advantaged instruments. If executed correctly, life insurance (and its investment components) can be not only tax-advantaged, it can be tax-*free!*

Let's review the three categories of investments. Probably the most familiar are *taxable* accounts, including investments such as savings accounts, CDs, regular brokerage accounts, mutual funds, and real estate. Also familiar are *tax-deferred* accounts such as IRAs, 401(k) plans, annuities, and pension plans. (Because of their familiarity, this chapter will not detail taxable and tax-deferred investment options.)

Perhaps least understood are the investment options within the *tax-free* category. There are only five—and most investors have only three of those available to them. Tax-free investments include the following:

1. Municipal bonds: These instruments earn tax-free interest. They represent a valid option for building the 30% tax-free wealth in a 30-40-30 mix (as shown in Figure 3). But municipal bonds can be too conservative an approach for most investors—especially those seeking long-term growth.

2. Roth IRAs: These individual retirement accounts are great if you can get them. If you earn too much annually, however, you are ineligible for them. If you do qualify, you are limited to a $4,000 annual contribution (according to 2007 tax laws). Still, this may be a useful tool for tax-free wealth accumulation.

3. 529 plans: These investment options allow parents (and grandparents) to accumulate money in tax-free accounts as part of their children's (or grandchildren's) college savings. This investment avenue is great for your kids or grandkids, but the money accrued is not really *your* money. It is your beneficiaries' money.

4. The equity in your principal residence: You can take up to $250,000 of equity in your home ($500,000 if you are married) in tax-free retirement income. This approach works well for those who will downsize when the kids move out or those who don't mind packing up and moving every few years. This tax-free accumulation technique is often overlooked. But most people plan to live in their current homes in retirement, so the home-equity option makes sense only for those who are willing to move from their homes in order to access tax-free dollars.

Take a wild guess what number 5 is. You got it!

5. Life insurance: Specifically, a *cash-value life insurance policy.*

I wish there were another name for this, in case you still have a negative mind-set about life insurance despite what you have read thus far in this book. So just for fun, let's not call it life insurance. Let's call this fifth approach for accumulating tax-free wealth something else. Let's call this investment opportunity the "other account." Did you know you could do the following with an "other account"?

- Deposit large cash amounts—more than a Roth or 401(k) or any qualified retirement plan allows—for almost unlimited accumulation potential.

- Allow the money to grow tax-deferred.

- Access the principal first—tax-free.

- Access the earnings via loans—tax-free.

- Borrow your money at zero interest rates or at very low rates, depending on the company that issues this "other account."

- Invest the money in guaranteed fixed accounts or into a wide range of bond and stock accounts.

- Move the money from one investment account to another with no fees or taxes.

Despite these features of an "other account," you still may be thinking, But it's insurance; the costs are high. To you I reply, The costs are inevitably higher for a good parachute compared with a discounted one. The costs are higher on a Lexus than a Yugo.

And so it is that in a properly structured "other account," *the cost of insurance is less than the tax in a comparable taxable account.*

Repeat out loud with me:

The cost of insurance is less than the tax in a comparable taxable account.

Third time:

The cost of insurance is less than the tax in a comparable taxable account.

You get my drift here? If you can use an "other account" to build up tax-free wealth *and* your cost is less than the taxes for your taxable investments *and* you can use a combination of guaranteed fixed accounts, bond accounts, and equity accounts to offset your investment risks, why wouldn't you take advantage?

Perhaps your answer is that you simply did not know life insurance offered such a broad and flexible range of benefits. Perhaps the reason you did not know is that your financial advisers did not apprise you of this fact. Then again, you may have been apprised, but you just didn't believe the advice given. You may have been trapped in old myths discussed in Chapter 2.

Adopting open minds, let's contemplate some possibilities that might lie ahead for you. Imagine putting large dollar amounts into a cash-value policy and letting it grow tax-deferred for 15 years or so. At that point, you take out your principal tax-free and then take earnings out tax-free via no-cost loans. Even better, you can leave the principal and earnings in the account to grow and compound tax-deferred for 30 or 40 years. Wouldn't it be great to have an account providing you with tax-free earnings to complement the taxable income from your 401(k) or IRA investments?

Unfortunately, the vast majority of investors have portfolios that look more like Figure 2, with a disproportionate bucket of tax-deferred money. Now, a big tax-deferred bucket is a good thing. Having a lot of money in an IRA at retirement is better than not. But by improving your tax diversification, you allow yourself greater flexibility in how you realize your income in retirement.

Tax
Diversification

● ● ● ●

Two examples in the following table illustrate the effects of limited tax diversification versus well-balanced tax diversification.

	Example 1	Example 2
Annual income desired	$ 60,000	$ 60,000
Source of funds	IRAs and taxable savings	Equal distribution of investments across the three tax categories
Tax rate	30%	30%*
Amount needed before tax (to create the $60,000 of income desired)	$ 85,715	$78,000

* Note: Because 30% of the income is tax-free, the 30% tax rate is assessed only against the 70% of the retirement income that is taxable and tax-deferred. Some taxable income might be at capital gains rates and thus less than illustrated.

Example 2 represents an annual tax savings of $7,715 compared with Example 1. Do the math. Over a retirement of 25 years, the total tax savings come close to a quarter of a million dollars! Moreover, the tax-free accounts would have grown faster than taxable investments because of the power of tax-free compounding features.

You may be concerned that you cannot earn a decent return, net after expenses, in a life insurance policy. That is untrue. You can earn certificate-type returns in universal life policies, and you can earn similar returns to a diversified stock and bond portfolio (or diversified mutual fund portfolio) with a variable universal life policy. Yes, there are costs. In a well-funded policy, however, you can net excellent returns on your invested dollars, even after the costs involved. You have the death benefit in the event you die prematurely—and you have real, accessible investment dollars in retirement. You don't have to die to make these policies work nicely for you.

Ginny and Robert's Story:

Ginny and Robert saved diligently for their retirement. After many years at a national computer company, they retired together with sizable amounts accumulated in their 401(k) and pension plans. Before retirement, their combined annual income was $190,000. They believed that a retirement income of $150,000 annually would allow them to continue their current lifestyle throughout retirement. With pensions of $3,900 a month for Ginny and $3,400 a month for Robert, along with 401(k) balances of $1,285,000, they calculated their annual retirement income, as follows:

Pension income:	$ 87,600
401(k) income: $1,285,000 @ 5%:	$ 64,250
Annual income:	$151,850

Unfortunately, the couple overlooked the tax consequences of this income stream, which continues the calculation, as follows:

Subtract 30% estimated income tax:	($45,555)
Net annual income:	$106,295

Because all of Ginny and Robert's income and investments were taxable, their retirement goals were grossly underfunded. They did not have the luxury of accessing tax-free accounts.

This news calls for a headline: In a well-funded policy, you can earn similar, if not higher, net returns on invested dollars than in a comparable taxable account.

Mind you, dozens of disclaimers and "yeah, buts" require discussion with your financial advisers before you apply for a permanent policy.[3] For now, simply consider that if you have a purpose for life insurance (and remember it could be a thousand different reasons as discussed in Chapter 3), diversifying some of your investment dollars into a permanent policy can make great sense.

> In a well-funded policy, you can earn similar, if not higher, net returns on invested dollars than in a comparable taxable account.

Life insurance provides one of the most effective ways legally to avoid income taxes on the cash accumulation *and* the death benefit. A cash-value insurance policy is analogous to a black hole in space. A black hole is very compact and possesses tremendous energy. Mysteriously, light goes in and never comes back out. Similarly, these policies are compact and contain powerful, wealth-generating features in one small package. The energy that can be generated within the policy is amazing. Instead of light going in, dollars go in. After the initial investment, if implemented properly, the IRS *never* sees the "light" of another penny in the account ... *ever*! As the cash values grow, they compound tax-deferred. With cash value accounts, taking profits, borrowing from tax-deferred earnings, or (in variable policies) moving money from one type of investment to another does not trigger a 1099 report. The IRS never sees these funds—thus, no taxation. Upon the death of the poli-

---

3   Before executing any insurance policy, you should first discuss the complexities involved with your financial adviser(s). You should be apprised of all sales charges, management fees on any subaccounts, mortality and expense fees, and all other policy fees that may apply. You should understand the time required to maintain a policy so that you avoid "surrender" charges. Moreover, you should be advised that unless you maintain appropriate cash levels, the policy may lapse, thereby rendering taxable any tax-free income previously received.

cyholder, any remaining value in the policy passes income tax-free to the policyholder's heirs.

Before leaving the topic of tax diversification, allow me to underscore one last important point. The discussions in this chapter and throughout this book summarize how the VUL investment strategy works in a *maximally* funded policy, which is what I urge my clients to establish whenever possible. I tell them that it is okay if they can't afford to fund maximally a permanent policy right now, as long as they can "catch up" later. But to underfund intentionally, I say to them *do not do it!* Instead, overfund by investing *more* than the minimum amounts established by the insurance company—or else do not buy these policies.

So are we agreed? Diversifying investments in the time and tax domains makes sense because we don't know the future—as it relates to our lives and as it relates to state and federal tax codes. But what if you can't afford to maximally fund a VUL, yet you need a substantial amount of coverage for your family and for future strategies? What should you do? Answers to those questions are the focus of the next chapter that discusses *term* versus *perm*—the battleground of the Titans. It is a bloody, painful place to venture, but let's face the battle together!

Rick and Tu's Story:

Rick and Tu saved diligently for their retirement. In fact, they earned exactly the same amounts in their pension accounts and 401(k) plans as Ginny and Robert (see opposite sidebar). In contrast to Ginny and Robert, however, Rick and Tu began accumulating money in tax-free positions over the many years. As soon as they qualified, they invested in Roth IRAs. They also invested in cash-value life insurance policies in each of their names, and they leveraged the tax-advantaged savings available within those policies. By retirement age, Rick and Tu had accumulated $874,000 tax-free, providing them an additional $43,705 in tax-free income annually—exactly the amount needed to arrive at their targeted income of $150,000 a year after taxes, as follows:

Pension income:	$ 87,600
401(k) income: $1,285,000 @ 5%:	$ 64,250
Annual income:	$151,850
Less 30% estimated income tax:	($45,555)
Tax-free income from life insurance policies: $874,000 @ 5%	$ 43,700
Net annual income:	$149,995

Voila! Rick and Tu experienced the power of tax diversification. By saving all they could in their 401(k) plans *and* by saving in tax-free investments, they built a comfortable retirement for themselves.

Questions to discuss with your financial advisers:

1. What percent of my assets are in each tax position: taxable, tax-deferred, and tax-free?

2. What strategies are available to me to create better tax diversification?

3. Since the cost of the insurance is less than the cost of taxes in a taxable account, why wouldn't I want to use a maximally funded VUL to build tax-free wealth?

4. How much of my current assets might be appropriately diversified into the tax-free instruments?

5. What if tax rates go up in the future? What are the implications for my current tax diversification?

5

The Term Versus Perm Battleground

Which is best—*term* or *perm*? This debate is a battleground of the ages—a clash between insurance industry "cultures": the "termites" versus the "whole-lifers"—term is cheap … whole life is guaranteed … And so it goes.

Here's an analogous scenario. Imagine that you are building a dog-house for Fido. You want both a hammer and a saw in your tool set, right? But two opposing groups of carpenters are screaming advice to you: "Hammers rule. Saws are stupid."

"No, you don't know what you're talking about. Saws are the answer. Hammers are outdated."

"Hammers work better, and they're cheaper!"

Well, our industry is engaged in a similarly silly debate on the term-versus-perm issue. Setting aside the chatter, let's get to the central question at hand: Which of these two approaches to life insurance will lead you and your family to a financially secure position?

My simple answer is: Both will. Indeed, permanent life insurance *and* traditional, pure term insurance have a place in nearly everyone's financial plan.

As I have stated previously, all financial advisers apply their biases in their professional practices. My biases are reflected in the following basic, three-step process through which I routinely guide clients as they establish the life insurance components of their comprehensive financial plans.

First, each client (couple) establishes a *range* of life insurance coverage that is appropriate for them. I ask my clients to determine the dollar amount they would need to maintain their current lifestyle in the event either spouse died. This "need amount" establishes the *absolute minimum* amount of life insurance they should have. Then I ask them to understand their economic human life value—the money a court would award the surviving spouse in the event of the other's wrongful death. The human life value establishes the *maximum* amount of life insurance the client should have. With a range established, I ask the clients to tell me where they want to fall within that range. Most choose a value in between, but leaning toward the higher human life value amount.

Next, with the desired coverage established, I explore with clients whether they can cover some or all of that amount with permanent insurance for its time diversification benefits (discussed in Chapter 3) as well as its tax diversification advantages (discussed in Chapter 4). I encourage them to start with as much permanent insurance as they can reasonably afford—calculated in Step 3.

Last, to establish the most cost-effective permanent policy, I guide clients to purchase a death-benefit amount that is the smallest amount of permanent coverage allowed by the maximum amount they are willing to invest. Let me further explain this approach.

The IRS knows that permanent life insurance policies represent a significant tax break, and so it imposes certain limitations. The IRS establishes how much can be invested in a permanent policy based on the size of the death benefit payout. Ideally, a client will take full advantage—up to the maximum tax shelter allowed. Typically, the maximum shelter is determined by the assets moved from taxable accounts or from extra, discretionary cash flow each month. After determining how much can and should be allocated, we calculate the size of the death benefit—ideally, the smallest benefit allowed while maintaining all the tax benefits and keeping costs low over time. (This approach is consistent with the "flying the plane full" analogy discussed in Chapter 2). For example, if the clients have determined that the desired amount of coverage is $1.5 million but can maximally fund only $250,000, we establish a $250,000 permanent life insurance policy supplemented by $1.25 million of convertible term insurance. If the clients have very little discretionary cash flow and a large insurance need, I recommend an investment *entirely* in term insurance. Conversely, if the clients have available funds in repositionable assets or in cash flow or in a combination of both to fully fund a $1.5 million permanent policy, I recommend a "no term, all perm" policy.

In my professional experience, I have observed that minimally funded permanent policies can lead to three negative outcomes. First, a minimally funded permanent policy will not grow appreciably because tax-deferred compounding will be very limited. Second, the minimally funded policy will be subject to extreme pressure in a declining market, which could cause clients to pay in more premiums—perhaps at a time they can least afford to, at which point they have to drop their coverage altogether. Third, minimally funded permanent policies often cause clients to settle for less coverage than they should have. I counsel my clients that it is far better to carry the full coverage amount (in this example, $1.5 million) in term insurance than to settle for less (say, $600,000) of underfunded permanent coverage.

Chuck and Terry's Story

A year and half ago, Chuck and Terry, a couple in their mid-40s, purchased term insurance as part of their comprehensive financial plan. They purchased a $700,000 policy on Terry, a manager at a shipping company, and a $500,000 policy on Chuck, who at the time was starting a new consulting company. The two amounts represented the low end of their need-versus-human-life-value continuum. Given the costs and risks associated with Chuck's start-up, however, the couple could afford to insure only the family's basic needs—and they certainly could not afford higher premiums associated with a permanent policy.

That eventually changed. A recent review reveals that much has improved in Chuck and Terry's financial profile. Chuck's business has not just taken off, it is thriving. Chuck's annual gross income is $150,000—an amount he conservatively estimates will grow by $25,000 to $50,000 over the next several years. Consequently, the couple is reconfiguring their insurance policies. Terry is increasing her coverage up to $1 million (a reflection that her human life value is more than that amount), and she is changing to a 50/50 mix of term and permanent insurance. Chuck's human life value has increased dramatically—commensurate with his economic value to his family. Moreover, he now has the ability to save for the future by funding a permanent policy. Therefore, Chuck will carry a $1.5 million permanent policy and will increase his term coverage up to $1 million. This amount for Chuck is higher than the amount the family needs to pay their bills in the untimely event of his death—but the amount is well below his full human life value.

Chuck and Terry plan to meet periodically with their financial planners to explore their coverage amounts and to adjust them accordingly as their economic situation changes over time.

When cash flow limitations dictate term insurance purchases, I counsel clients to only buy term that is *convertible* to some excellent permanent policies. As more money becomes available to them (such as through increased salary, bonuses, stock options, or inheritances), clients then can contemplate reallocating their investments. Following the principles of tax diversification discussed in Chapter 4—30% into taxable accounts, 40% into tax-deferred accounts, and 30% into tax-free accounts—the clients who had purchased $1.5 million of convertible term might later convert $300,000 of the term to a permanent policy, keeping $1.2 million of the term insurance in place. Those same clients, upon realizing that with increased income their human life value had also increased, might elect to keep the full term policy in place and add another $300,000 of permanent coverage on top.

So getting back to the battleground, you might ask what circumstances have led to this contrived controversy. The answer is that many financial advisers are licensed or trained to sell only one type of insurance product. The newer, more complex products require more licenses. (In addition to state insurance licenses, variable products require securities licenses.) Moreover, these newer products require continuous attention and servicing. Much of the insurance industry is simply not prepared to provide the annual service and advice required to manage properly all types of policies. Consequently, financial professionals tend to fight for "their" turf. They adopt the attitude, "If I can't sell it, or if I won't service it, I'll just badmouth it." The media fuels the controversy with their lack of technical knowledge and their love of controversy. The "information" offered in daily newspapers and weekly magazines may be well-intentioned, but it is almost always wrong.

Sadly, nothing about this term-versus-perm controversy serves you, the consumer. You need counsel from advisers who offer a full range of financial products and life insurance solutions. Additionally, you need periodic (at least annual) review of your portfolio for changes in your cash flow, risk planning, tax planning, estate planning, and other investment goals. You also need professional guidance to review regularly how your investment products are performing in relation to current interest rates, stock and bond market returns, insurance costs, and dividends declared.

Here is my overarching advice to you: As you build your "house" of financial independence, choose a financial "carpenter" who works with a full set of tools, knows how to use them skillfully, and knows when to apply one versus the other to optimize your financial profile.

In conclusion, *term* versus *perm*? Both!

Questions to discuss with your financial advisers:

1. What is your personal and professional opinion of term insurance versus permanent insurance?

2. Are you limited in any way from selling me the full range of life insurance products available in the marketplace? Are you licensed to sell variable products?

3. Would you mind sharing, without specific numbers, how you personally fill your own life insurance needs? Do you use term, permanent, or both? Why?

4. If you don't deal with the insurance side of financial planning [adviser deals with investments only], would you refer me to an insurance professional who has the full range of insurance products available and is open to both term and permanent approaches?

6

Life Insurance for the Stay-at-Home Spouse

The subtitle of this book could have been *You Are Grossly Underinsured*—but my editor overruled a long title. One of the main reasons I know that this statement—you are grossly underinsured—is most likely true for you is that for many American families the tremendous economic contributions of the stay-at-home spouse are largely overlooked. This oversight occurs by consumers, not to mention most financial services professionals.

So let's first establish what should be an obvious fact: The stay-at-home spouse provides a tremendous economic value to the family. I am not talking about some squishy, politically correct notion here. I am talking about quantifiable dollars and cents. Take a look at Table 1, which provides a partial list of the roles and tasks performed by the stay-at-home spouse, to see what I mean.

Table 1. Estimated annual economic contribution of the stay-at-home spouse.

Job Description Total	Wage	Annual
Babysitting	45 hours/week @ $ 8/hour x 50 weeks	$ 18,000
Driving	10 hours/week @ $12/hour x 50 weeks	$ 6,000
Tutoring	10 hours/week @ $12/hour x 40 weeks	$ 4,800
Meal Preparation	15 hours/week @ $10/hour x 52 weeks	$ 7,800
Cleaning	15 hours/week @ $10/hour x 52 weeks	$ 7,800
Other	10 hours/week @ $10/hour x 52 weeks	$ 5,200
	TOTAL	$ 49,600

You may be thinking that the numbers add up to far more hours than your spouse puts in each week on such work. That thought leads to my first point: Your spouse, like most, is a multitasker! That said, a larger point here is that it would cost roughly the amounts listed in the table to hire others to do all the tasks now performed by your stay-at-home spouse.

If you are not convinced, ask yourself: If I could hire one person who could really do all these things—sit, drive, tutor cook, clean, do errands, do the marketing, repair things—how much would this phenomenal person charge? Answer: $50,000 a year would be a bargain.

Or you may already be convinced. You may have looked at the estimates in Table 1 and thought, This guy is crazy if he thinks we can get a decent babysitter-cook-driver-tutor-whatever for those hourly amounts.

Which brings us to the "so what" of this discussion. The economic contribution of the stay-at-home spouse to the typical American family with children living in the household is at least $50,000 a year. If you add inflation and multiply the amounts by the number of years the kids are around (say 18–25 years), the economic loss suffered if the stay-at-home spouse were to die could be as high as $1.25 million.

Actually, my $50,000 a year estimate is on the conservative side. One Web site (salary.com) places the value at over $134,000 a year. This figure may not be realistic in most cases, but the point remains the same: American stay-at-home spouses are grossly underinsured.

Headline: The economic value of the stay-at-home spouse can easily be $1.25 million over time.

I hope that, based on the foregoing discussion, you are now asking a series of questions, such as:

- How much life insurance do we have on the spouse whose work is to stay home and take care of the kids and the household?

- Have we adequately accounted for the real economic value— the economic contributions made?

- Are we prepared to hire out all these duties with quality, well-trained personnel in the event this spouse dies unexpectedly?

I also hope that you are questioning how this shortfall in your life insurance coverage escaped your attention—why your financial advisers haven't brought up this issue for your consideration.

Recall from previous chapters that financial services professionals carry strong biases against life insurance, which makes it difficult for them to see the potential economic value of the stay-at-home spouse as clearly as you now see it. Indeed, many advisers may be locked into one way of viewing their clients' financial situations, unable to gain a fresh perspective—which reminds me of the old-lady-young-lady experiment, illustrated in the sidebar discussion.

Old Lady? Young Lady?

Perhaps you have seen this picture before. It was part of a famous psychology experiment in which the picture was shown to two groups of college students. One group was told that the picture depicted an old lady—an old hag with a crook nose. The other group was told that the picture was of a young lady—a beautiful 1920s flapper with a stylish, feathered hat. Then the two groups were brought together to debate their perceptions. The first group, of course, saw only the old hag. The second group vehemently defended their view that the picture, in fact, depicted a beautiful young lady.

The debate seems silly, doesn't it? We know that both perceptions are possible. The picture represents both an old lady and a young lady—depending on how you view it.

As in this example, we humans see only what we see. Most financial advisers tend to see the "old lady" aspects of financial need. That is, they are trained to think only of how much a family will need to get by if a breadwinner were to die. They are trained to calculate what percentage of current living expenses will need to be covered in the event a breadwinner dies. In the vast majority of cases, the focus is on the income of the spouse who works outside the home. The standard assumption is that in the event the stay-at-home spouse dies, no economic need arises because the source of income from the "working spouse" is intact.

Financial plans abound that are based on this assumption—viewing only the "old lady" side of the picture. Indeed, for years my own financial plan ignored the financial impact if my wife, Val, had met an untimely death during the years she stayed at home to raise our children and manage our household. Our thinking was that I was the one earning the income. If Val were to die, the family income would continue so there was no "need" to insure Val's life. But our limited perspective ignored the "young lady" side of the equation—the human life value inherent in Val's economic contributions to our household. If Val had died when she was serving as the stay-at-home spouse, our family might not have experienced economic "need"—but we most certainly would have been dealt a huge economic loss (not to mention all the other losses suffered).

So which is it: "old lady" or "young lady"—economic need or human life value? By now you know the answer: Both!

If your advisers cannot see the human life value aspects of your financial situation, help them out. Initiate the discussion yourself. Together you can decide whether to insure all or part of the human life value inherent in the contributions made by the stay-at-home spouse. Make a *conscious* decision, knowing its implications and taking full responsibility.

So far we have considered only the direct economic impact on a young family when a stay-at-home parent dies. In deciding the conditions and the appropriate amount of life insurance, other aspects of this topic deserve contemplation.

Like Raj (in the example sidebar stories), imagine that your stay-at-home spouse has died, leaving you, the primary wage earner, alone with the children. Further, imagine that the life insurance you purchased covered your spouse's full human life value—providing enough money to hire all the help you need to manage the household and care for the children. Is the amount really enough? Perhaps it is—and then again, perhaps you can envision other possibilities. Instead of jumping back in to full-time work, maybe you want to stay home several months or longer—both to deal with your loss and to help the kids with the difficult transition. Alternatively, maybe you want to continue to work, but to work shorter days and to take more days off.

How much would cutting back your work schedule affect your income—10%, 25%, or more? It is hard to imagine how you'd react until you had to face such a situation. So doesn't it make sense to give yourself the *option* not to have to work for a time by adequately insuring the life of your spouse now?

So we've established at least two valid reasons to insure the stay-at-home spouse:

- To cover the economic contributions of the stay-at-home spouse to the household

- To provide funds to allow the surviving spouse to take time off from work after the death of the stay-at-home spouse

---

Raj and Rene's Story

Raj never insured Rene. As the sole breadwinner of the family, he never saw the need to insure her.

Both age 35, the couple had three children all living at home. Raj managed his own successful small business while Rene stayed at home running the household and taking care of the children. Suddenly, without warning, Rene died of a brain aneurism, leaving Raj with the business, the household, the kids—not to mention the emotional pain of no wife and no mother for his children.

Now, four months since Rene's death, Raj finds himself trying to balance the demands at work with the complex, unending needs of his children and the hundreds of details Rene once handled each week to operate the household smoothly. Simply stated, life is not working. Raj is unable to get everything done. He is depressed, finding no time to grieve his loss. His business is suffering. His kids are struggling. He has tried hiring babysitters, housecleaners, and tutors—but the piecemeal approach results in too many details being left undone. He has hired more staff to make up for his inattention to the business, but his income continues to decline. Raj feels himself falling apart, and he does not know what to do. He desperately needs time off, but can't afford to take it.

Yet other reasons require consideration in establishing the conditions and coverage amounts for insuring the life of the stay-at-home spouse. Such reasons include:

- Providing coverage for the stay-at-home spouse in the event of divorce.

  Not a pleasant thought, but it happens. Doesn't it make sense for the stay-at-home spouse to own some of the coverage in the event of divorce? Otherwise, the working spouse could change the beneficiary or cancel the policy, leaving the "nonworking" spouse without coverage. (By the way, if you are a stay-at-home spouse in the midst of an impending divorce, be sure you gain ownership of any existing life insurance as part of your settlement.)

- Creating a personal pension plan for the stay-at-home spouse. Most, if not all, of the retirement money will accrue to the spouse who earns income. Wouldn't you, the stay-at-home spouse, feel more financially secure if you had your own retirement dollars accrued? If you were eligible, you could use IRAs and Roth IRAs. You could also use a *permanent* life insurance policy to build tax-advantaged savings for the future. At retirement, you could draw tax-free income from your life insurance policy to supplement other sources of income.

Raj and Rene's Story *(revised)*

Raj and Rene were thriving—he as the owner of a lucrative small business and she as the stay-at-home mother of their three young children. In addition to a $2 million life insurance policy on Raj, the couple also purchased a $1 million policy on Rene. The couple recognized that life insurance could make a huge difference in the event Rene died while the kids were still living at home.

Then the unexpected happened. Rene died suddenly of a brain aneurism. While Raj and his children continue to grieve their loss of wife, mother, and homemaker, they have had the luxury of a *tax-free,* $1 million cash infusion that has allowed them to do the following:

Raj has taken two months away from the business to stay home with his children. He could withstand a financial hit to his business with the buffer of tax-free money provided by Rene's insurance policy. During this two-month period, Raj has focused his time on the children—time they all needed to grieve. They were even able to take two expensive vacations during this time period.

Raj has hired a full-time, live-in housekeeper and nanny for an annual salary of $40,000 plus benefits and a car. The funds provided by Rene's insurance policy made it possible to hire this one professional who completes most of the daily chores required to care for the children and run the household.

Raj has had the funds available to hire a consulting firm to perform a comprehensive search for a great "right arm" business assistant. This search process was very expensive—but well-justified because in the long run, Raj will be able to work a normal 40- to 45-hour week, allowing him more time to be with his children in the evenings and on weekends.

In this revised scenario, the possibilities and choices abound for Raj and his children as they continue to grieve the loss of Rene. The aftermath to her death is greatly improved for her surviving family members.

- Creating a legacy for your kids or grandkids.
  You may want to insure your life so that when you die, your children (or grandchildren) will receive life insurance proceeds that allow them to live with financial independence.

The vast majority of American stay-at-home spouses are grossly under-insured. You may have sensed this fact, but until reading this chapter didn't know how to quantify your own situation. Now you do. This realization doesn't mean you have to run out and buy the $1.25 million coverage mentioned at the beginning of this chapter—an amount that may be too much, or it may be too little.

Instead, your fresh insights should lead you to have frank dialogue with your financial advisers. As I have warned in previous chapters, be prepared to meet resistance from your advisers who may view your situation simplistically—that is, solely from the need perspective. True, in your case, there may be no need in the traditional sense of paying the mortgage and feeding the kids. But the life of the stay-at-home spouse in your partnership has value—real, quantifiable, financial value.

As most of us strive to achieve financial independence, some Americans have already arrived there. The wealthy's reasons for owning life insurance may be very different. In the next chapter, we'll look at some of the same reasons the wealthy are underinsured, and we'll add some new reasons they should be looking at insurance as a possible solution for a new set of problems that comes with wealth in America.

Questions to ask your financial adviser:

1. Why am I, as the stay-at-home spouse, not worth insuring?

2. How would the premature death of our family's stay-at-home spouse have an adverse impact on our family? Or conversely, how would additional life insurance coverage have a positive impact on our family?

3. Why would we insure our car but not insure an asset as valuable to the family as the stay-at-home spouse?

4. What is the economic value of the stay-at-home spouse in our family?

7

Life Insurance for the Wealthy Family

If your estate is currently under $3 million, you are not allowed to read this chapter. Just kidding! Actually, the fact is that we Americans are all headed in the direction of becoming multimillionaires—or at least our kids are headed there. Either way, this chapter carries relevance for you. Read on.

For the family with a high net worth, the overarching financial challenge is *estate preservation* when ownership of the estate passes from one person to another. Indeed, the costs associated with dying are high—costs that require liquidity if the beneficiaries are to meet the tax burdens imposed by present-day tax codes. The question to ask yourself at this juncture is whether your estate will have enough *liquid* dollars at the time of your death to ensure that it is left intact for your beneficiaries—your heirs and charitable organizations.

In my professional life, I have had the opportunity to observe and to advise the investment habits of many wealthy individuals. I note that these people follow at least two common principles that guide their investment behaviors. First, they understand and apply the power of *leverage*. They leverage the work of others when they own businesses, and they leverage debt when they buy real estate property. Consequently, they turn pennies into dollars.

Second, the wealthy people I have observed understand the importance of *minimizing taxes at every opportunity.* They seek professional advice from financial advisers, tax accountants, and tax attorneys in determining the least amount of tax required of them by law. They realize that each dollar not paid to Uncle Sam is another dollar of potential wealth that can be leveraged to earn more dollars.

Life insurance meets these two wealth-building principles: tax minimization and leverage. By its very nature, insurance is leverage in that policyholders pay less than the dollars they receive in return. In well-designed policies, the leverage can be substantial. Moreover, life insurance represents one of the best tax-planning strategies available to wealth-builders. Investing in life insurance offers the following tax advantages:

- The cash values in permanent life insurance policies grow tax-deferred.

- Cash accumulations can be accessed tax-free in either of two ways: (1) by withdrawing from the principal amount invested or (2) by taking out low-cost or zero-cost loans against the earnings.

- The death benefits paid to beneficiaries are tax-free.

To review: *tax-deferred* growth … *tax-free* withdrawals … *tax-free* death benefits.

To repeat: *tax-deferred* growth … *tax-free* withdrawals … *tax-free* death benefits.

(I have been telling you that life insurance is fun! What could be more fun than saving on taxes? See Chapter 4 for detailed discussion on the topic.)

Ultimately, we each arrive at this fundamental choice: To pay a modest amount to the insurance companies for the tax-free, wealth-building instruments they provide—or to pay *a lot* to the federal government. Which will it be for you—insurance company or the IRS? You decide.

New clients who come to me for advice most often possess one glaring gap in their financial profiles. Typically, they have placed the lion's share of their amassed wealth in retirement accounts, such as IRAs or 401(k) accounts, that name the surviving spouse as the primary beneficiary. (See Shirley and Will's story in the sidebar as an example.) Retirement accounts certainly offer some excellent tax advantages in that they defer the tax bill to a future date. But any wealthy couple disproportionately invested in retirement accounts is missing huge opportunities for *tax-free* investing. My advice to them is to plan ahead so they will be able to fund a *bypass trust* as part of their living trust. Very few American couples with living trusts have planned for the liquid cash needed to fund a bypass trust at the time the first of the two spouses dies. For the typical American family, a house and some retirement money make up the majority of the assets—assets assigned to the surviving spouse, not to the bypass trust. Such families simply do not have enough liquid money available to put into a trust at the time the first spouse dies.

A bypass trust is an investment strategy that allows *both* A and B sides of the trust to pass through to the heirs without incurring estate tax, regardless of which spouse dies first. Also called an *exemption trust, B-trust,* or *below-ground trust,* a bypass trust allows the trustees to claim their "exemption amount" at the time of the "first death" of the spouses, according to a written estate plan. The funded amount in this bypass trust transfers estate-tax-free to the beneficiaries of the estate upon the death of the second spouse. The amount in the bypass trust can grow to any size and still escape estate taxation. Ideally, a husband and wife would each want to fully fund the exemption amount at the first death (no matter which spouse died first). The following table summarizes the exemption amounts according to U.S. tax codes in effect in 2007.

Exemptions and Maximum Tax Rates I		
Year	Estate Tax Exemption	Highest Rate
2007	$2 million	45%
2008	$2 million	45%
2009	$3.5 million	45%
2010	N/A (taxes eliminated)	0%
2011	$1 million	55%

Shirley and Will's Story

In their late 60s, Shirley and Will believed that they were "set" financially. They had established a living trust. They owned a home valued at $1 million, her $2 million IRA, his $500,000 IRA, several cars with a total value of more than $300,000, in addition to household property, personal valuables, and ample cash. When Shirley died, the house, cars, and personal valuables went to Will (the A side of the trust). Shirley's $2 million IRA also went to Will, who was named as the primary beneficiary. Of course Will's IRA continued to be his as well as all the other assets the couple had amassed together. Ten years later, when Will died, the couple's heirs faced a huge tax liability on the estate. The couple had paid only $100,000 into Shirley's side of their bypass trust, which left $1.9 million of Shirley's IRA subject to taxation upon Will's death. The tax bill for this faulty financial planning was a hefty 43%—that is, $817,000 that was paid to the IRS instead of to Will and Shirley's children and grandchildren. Moreover, the $1.9 million that could have gone into the bypass trust would have compounded into many millions of dollars for the benefit of the couple's heirs.

You may ask, What is the vehicle of choice for funding a bypass trust? The answer is life insurance. Like Shirley and Will, many couples

Designed specifically to provide liquidity to heirs who may face considerable estate tax burdens when the "second spouse" of a couple dies. Such policies may include whole life, universal life, or variable life. Some policies combine term with some type of permanent insurance. The insurance industry uses the terms *last-to-die and second-to-die* interchangeably with first-to-die policies.

would be well-advised to purchase life insurance to fund the bypass trust when the first of the spouses dies. Alternatively, if financially unable to fund a bypass trust at "first death," couples may consider purchasing a *second-to-die* insurance policy (sometime also called a *last-to-die* policy) to pay the tax liability faced by the heirs when the second spouse dies.

Of course, paying estate taxes is not entirely avoidable. Paying *some* estate tax may be inevitable. Here again, many wealthy couples, without proper professional guidance, figure simply that some of the money in their retirement accounts will cover their estate tax burdens. But let's go through one calculation to reveal the error in their thinking. Let's consider the case of a large estate that incurs an estate tax of $1 million. The beneficiaries take the required money from an IRA worth $2 million. Subsequently, the IRS extracts *income* tax on the $1 million cash distribution—income tax to the tune of $300,000. That's not the end of it. Next, the $300,000 taken from the IRA to cover the income tax bill incurs another income tax of $90,000, for which the cash distribution from the IRA incurs an additional $30,000 income tax bill. Do the math and you find that the IRS took $1.4 million, leaving the estate only $600,000 of the original $2 million. I hope you're asking, Wouldn't buying a life insurance policy have been far less expensive? (I'm sure you know my answer.)

Thus far, we have talked about the leverage and tax-minimization advantages of life insurance. But there is an important third advantage: *liquidity*, which actually relates to the first two. Freeing up nontaxable cash becomes especially important when the investment objective is to provide equitable amounts to multiple heirs in complex situations—such as when one heir will take over a family-owned business that represents a disproportionate share of the estate's worth. In such instances, life insurance provides a simplified and efficient path to liquidity and to "evening out" an estate. (See *Phil's Story* on page 4.)

Additionally, the liquidity advantages of life insurance become important in "blended" families in which multiple heirs are generated by more than one marriage. For these families, life insurance provides a simplified means of distributing the assets of an estate across beneficiaries in the manner designated by the benefactors.

Furthermore, the liquidity of life insurance can facilitate revisions in investment strategies, if indicated, when the "first death" in a couple occurs. For example, tax-free, liquid dollars at the time the first spouse dies might be used by the surviving spouse to pay estate taxes (or capital gains taxes) *strategically* sooner on a rapidly appreciating asset. In a similar vein, tax-free liquid dollars from life insurance might be applied to a Roth conversion—that is, converting a regular IRA into a Roth IRA and thereby shifting *forever* taxable dollars into tax-free dollars. Dollars invested in a Roth IRA could magnify many times over the wealth passed through to the heirs. Life insurance provides the liquid funds needed to pay the taxes required at the time of conversion—allowing the IRA to grow unencumbered by taxation for the life of the account.

To review, wealth-conscious people invest in life insurance for several wealth-building (and wealth-preservation) reasons: leverage, tax minimization, and liquidity. Probably the overarching reason the wealthy invest in life insurance is for its flexibility in the face of an unpredictable future—a future for which none of us can know how changes in income tax rates, estate tax laws, and other fiscal factors will affect us financially. Because the future is unknowable, I advise my clients to *diversify* their investments and to place at least 5% of their wealth toward the tax-free, leveraged flexibility of a life insurance policy—a rule of thumb I think relevant to families with already amassed fortunes as well as those families well on their way to financial freedom.

I hope the concepts introduced in this chapter have convinced you that wealthy people need life insurance too. In fact, they may need it more than others. Fashioning a comprehensive investment strategy is best achieved with a professional team including (but not limited to) a financial planner, tax accountant, and tax attorney. The modest costs associated with assembling such a team could reap substantial monetary gains for the ultimate benefit of your heirs and your charitable concerns.

Questions to ask your financial adviser:

1. Do we have the liquidity to properly fund both sides of our bypass trusts if we both died tomorrow?

2. Does our estate have the liquidity to pay estate taxes without devastating nonliquid assets (like real estate, closely owned businesses, and retirement funds) at the time of our deaths?

3. Have we resolved issues of second marriages, special-needs children or grandchildren, uneven estate distribution associated with business holdings, and the like?

4. Would it make sense to give our retirement funds to nonprofit organizations and use life insurance instead to provide inheritances for our children and grandchildren?

5. Should we consider using life insurance to create an enduring legacy for our family or for our charitable concerns?

8

Freedom and Responsibility— "Bookends" for Life

To carry adequate life insurance is a moral obligation incumbent upon the great majority of citizens.

—Franklin Roosevelt

This book is driven by an underlying value that most (if not all) of us share: personal freedom—a value central to the framing of the U.S. Constitution. *A belief in and a commitment to individual freedom* lies at the very core of what defines being American.

One potential outgrowth of individual freedom is *financial* freedom— the freedom to earn a high standard of living and to live a life free from money worries. Isn't that what we all want, to reach a point at which all is well financially, where we are providing the good life for our families and ourselves?

Throughout life we are instructed by the universal laws of cause and effect—that by taking responsibility (cause), we gain our personal freedom (desired effect). For example, as children, to the extent that we rely on our parents to care for us, our personal freedoms are restricted. As adults, to the extent that we rely on our government to provide for us, we forfeit certain personal liberties. When we accept complete *responsibility* for our choices—our mistakes as well as our triumphs— we are on the path to generating personal *freedom* for ourselves.

In *Man's Search for Meaning*, author Viktor Frankl suggests that the Statue of Liberty on the East Coast of the United States be countered with a Statue of Responsibility on the West Coast. In fact, the Statue of Responsibility Foundation (sorfoundation.org) is working to meet Frankl's challenge. For me, the vision of these two statues is like a pair of bookends buttressing our nation.

Based on the premise that freedom derives from responsibility, this final chapter is a last call for responsible *action* on your part. Specifically, I am challenging you to complete the following five action items:

- Action 1: Schedule an appointment with a qualified financial adviser.

- Action 2: Consult with your financial adviser(s).

- Action 3: Initiate the underwriting process.

- Action 4: Activate your insurance policy.

- Action 5: Review your insurance coverage with your adviser(s) at least once a year.

Let's consider each of these actions in further detail.

◆　　　◆　　　◆

Action 1: Schedule an appointment. For most people, this first action is the hardest. Nonetheless, it is absolutely *the* most important. So whatever you are doing this moment, please stop and place a call. Even if this moment is after business hours, call anyway. Leave a message saying that you wish to schedule an appointment. If you do not yet have a qualified adviser, you can narrow your search by looking for professional designations such as CFP, CLU, ChFC, LUTCF, or MSFS. In addition, you can ask friends to recommend an adviser who possesses the following characteristics: competent, experienced, understandable, and trustworthy. The adviser you choose should be competent, experienced, and *licensed* to offer *all* types of life insurance. Your adviser should be able to explain your options in ways that are readily understood. Moreover, your adviser should be trustworthy because this quality will be especially important if the technicalities of the financial industry and its product choices become too difficult to comprehend fully and when following certain recommendations call for a leap of faith on your part.

◆　　　◆　　　◆

Action 2: Consult with your adviser(s). Use the questions at the end of the preceding chapters that are relevant to your situation to guide your discussions. (Some of the key questions are reframed at the end of this chapter.) Address each topic, expressing your concerns, trepidations, and feelings. Ultimately, your discussions should lend clarity on the amounts of term versus permanent life insurance that are appropriate for you at this time.

◆　　　◆　　　◆

Action 3: Initiate the underwriting process. This third step is another huge hurdle for most people. This is the step where so many clients end an otherwise productive session by saying, "I need to think about it." When a financial adviser friend of mine hears these words, he leans back in his chair and stares at the ceiling. After a long pause, the client says, "Rick, what are you staring at?"

Rick responds, "I'm looking at the photos of all the people who said they would think about it and actually came back to *do something* about their financial situation." In actuality, there are no photos on Rick's office ceiling, and that's his point—perhaps a bit heavy-handed, but straightforwardly stated.

So if you are inclined to procrastinate, you might want to read Angela and Rico's Story (sidebar) and then consider that this action item carries a built-in grace period offering you time to "think about it." Typically, the underwriting process requires four to eight weeks. During this time you can think, study, fret, second-guess, call your friends, and meet with your advisers several more times as you process your decision. (If four weeks or longer isn't enough time for you to achieve closure on your insurance selection, you and your family are in big trouble!) Moreover, once you have your policy in hand you will still have ample opportunities to amend the policy—change funding levels, move more of the death benefit from term to permanent or from permanent to term, and so forth.

Angela and Rico's Story

Angela and Rico brought to their regularly scheduled financial planning meeting the joyful news that Angela was pregnant with their first child. They wished to explore the feasibility of Angela's being a stay-at-home mom while Rico worked to keep the family lifestyle intact. Because Rico had just received a nice promotion and raise, the timing seemed perfect. For the past two years, their financial adviser had voiced concerns that the couple was underinsured, but they said they wanted to wait until a baby came along before addressing the issue. Now, with a baby on the way, the adviser once again broached the subject. This time the couple agreed that more insurance made sense. Despite the adviser's recommendation that they complete an application in that session, however, Rico said that he wanted to wait until his return from an upcoming business trip.

For two months thereafter, the adviser placed several follow-up calls. Each time, Rico said he had something more pressing going on. Tragically, just nine weeks after the financial planning meeting, Rico was killed in an automobile accident. He died with only minimal group term benefits from a policy through his employer.

Now Angela is left without a husband, without a father for her child, and without financial options. She will have to return to work. On her income alone, she cannot afford to keep her home. The implications of Rico's and her procrastination resonate down the line: where Angela will live, how she will secure child care, where her child will attend school, how she will fund her child's college education and her own retirement, and every other lifestyle choice Angela will make as a single parent.

(Here again, if you choose a trustworthy adviser in the first action item, your anxieties should quickly dissipate.)

◆　　　◆　　　◆

Action 4: Activate your insurance policy. Before you sign on the dotted line, review the policy offer with your adviser, paying particular attention to costs, surrender charges, loan features, conversion privileges, and guarantees versus no guarantees.

At this stage, some clients are thrown off track by the news that the policy offered has been *rated*—meaning that the policy carries certain exclusions or added costs based on actuarial calculations indicating the purchaser may die earlier than the average life expectancy. Some people use this unwelcome news as an excuse not to accept the policy. In such cases, I advise my clients that they need life insurance *even more* than those who qualify for a "standard" (unrated) policy.

As soon as you and your adviser(s) determine that you understand and agree with the terms of the policy offered, *sign the documents.* Then take a moment to congratulate yourself. Feel proud of your responsible action. Even if at this stage you are not covered for your full human life value, you have moved yourself and your family in the right direction—further along the path toward financial freedom.

◆　　　◆　　　◆

Action 5: Review your insurance coverage at least once a year, every year. One constant in life is that every aspect is subject to change—income, unforeseen expenses, health status, family milestones, tax rates, and tax laws, to name just a few. For this reason, I review my clients' portfolios with them periodically—at least once every year. We reevaluate their need amount and their financial human life value, and we make adjustments accordingly. We assess the performance of investment accounts within their variable universal life policies and reallocate monies when indicated.

Conducting periodic reviews is what savvy financial advisers are paid to do—and insist that they do. Reflecting back to the first action item in this process, be sure you choose a financial adviser who commits to periodically reviewing your financial portfolio with you.

◆   ◆   ◆

Now you have five straightforward steps that make up a road map toward greater financial independence. If your response is to wait until "tomorrow" to begin the journey, you might reflect on the Frogs' Story (sidebar).

Frogs' Story

There once were four frogs sitting on a log. Three decided to jump off. How many were left sitting on the log?

No, not one. *Four.* Three frogs decided to jump, but that decision took place in their heads. They didn't actually jump. They merely decided to.

Aristotle said, "A is A," which was his way of saying *reality exists*. As in all aspects of life, "A is A" in financial planning. The reality is that someday each of us will die. Until that day, some of us will live 30, 40, or even 50 years in retirement. This reality dictates having a great deal of money if we are to live out our days in comfort and grace. (At least half of us will need long-term care as well—but that's a topic for another book.) Embracing an "A is A" philosophy is helpful in an ever-changing world. As tax laws change, if the estate tax is repealed then later reenacted, if a job is lost, if a spouse dies an untimely death, or if any number of unforeseen circumstances confront us, we can apply the "A is A" logic to guide our best decision-making in the moment. That's the best any of us can ever do in providing for ourselves and our families.

Life insurance increases the stability of the business world, raises its moral tone, and puts premium upon those habits of thrift and saving which are so essential to the welfare of the people as a body.

—Theodore Roosevelt

Choosing to purchase life insurance is a moral decision reflecting the value one places on taking responsibility. As greater numbers of us step up to living responsibly, we will enhance our personal as well as our collective freedoms in a million small and not so small ways. If we build (literally and figuratively) the Statue of Responsibility to complement the Statue of Liberty, we will improve our country and ourselves.

This book has been a call for taking responsible action on the path toward financial freedom. I have challenged you throughout to confront the reality of your own mortality and to *act* based on professional consultations from trusted advisers for your benefit and the benefit of those who depend on you. You have the choice to be grossly underinsured—or you can take action *today* to improve your financial condition. You are free to choose. It's the American way.

Questions to Ask Your Financial Adviser:

1. Will you commit to reviewing my insurance coverage with me periodically? (If the answers if no, consider finding a different adviser!)

2. What principles guide your professional judgments, actions, and advice?

3. What are some of your personal values that influence how you work with your clients?

4. How much life insurance do I need to sustain my family's current standard of living in the event of my death or my spouse's death? What is my current financial human life value? What is my spouse's? Should our coverage amounts approximate our human life value? (See Chapter 1.)

5. What is the long-term strategy for my life insurance? Does it serve a single purpose or many over time? How does my current coverage fit into this strategy? (See Chapter 2.)

6. Should we consider insuring our children, our parents, or our grandparents? (See Chapter 3.)

7. What strategies and investment instruments are available for diversifying our assets across three categories: taxable, tax-deferred, tax-free? (See Chapter 4.)

8. How much of the coverage on each of us should be term and how much should be permanent coverage? Should we use variable universal life for the long-term, tax-advantaged investment accumulation? If not, why not? (See Chapter 5.)

9. How would the premature death of our family's stay-at-home spouse have an adverse impact on our family? Or conversely, how would additional life insurance coverage have a positive impact on our family? (See Chapter 6.)

10. How should we fund the permanent (VUL) policy? Cash flow? Existing taxable assets that can be repositioned? Future bonuses or stock options exercised? How much liquidity should we create through life insurance? (See Chapter 7.)

11. In addition to life insurance, should we be looking at disability income insurance and long-term care coverage?

Glossary of Life Insurance Terminology

B-trust	See *bypass trust.*
Below-Ground Trust	See *bypass trust.*
Bypass Trust	Also called an *exemption trust*, *B-trust*, or *below-ground trust*, a bypass trust allows the trustees to claim their "exemption amount" at the time of the "first death" of the spouses, according to a written estate plan. The funded amount in this bypass trust transfers estate-tax-free to the beneficiaries of the estate upon the death of the second spouse. The amount in the bypass trust can grow to any size and still escape estate taxation.
Cash-Value Policy	Any form of permanent insurance, which means all forms of life insurance except term insurance. Cash-value policies have both the term insurance element and an additional cash accumulation element. Included in this category are whole life, universal life, death benefit guarantee universal life, and variable universal life. This term is analogous to the term *permanent insurance.*
Exemption Trust	See *bypass trust.*
First-to-Die Insurance	See *last-to-die-insurance.*
In-force Ledger	See *reprojection.*
Pension Maximization Strategy	Used for retirees faced with choosing among various monthly pension options—whether to take a higher amount each month, leaving their spouses with nothing when they die, or a reduced monthly amount, leaving continuing pensions to their survivors. An alternative approach to a reduced pension is to use life insurance to replace the pension amount in the event of death.
Permanent Insurance	Consists of both a term insurance element and a cash value accumulation. As the name implies, it is often intended to be used over the course of a lifetime until the time of death. Having permanent insurance is analogous to owning instead of renting a home throughout one's lifetime. Permanent insurance varies according to type: universal life, death benefit guarantee universal life, and variable universal life. This term is analogous to a *cash value policy.*
Second-to-Die Insurance	See *last-to-die insurance.*

About the Author

Ed Kelly began his career as a financial consultant in 1986. Now he is an owner in a financial planning firm in Los Angeles, California. Ed is frequently an invited speaker at industry conferences and events. He is regarded by other financial services professionals as a teacher and a coach. Ed is a devoted husband to his wife, Val, and is the proud father of their twins, Shannon and Stephen.

You can contact Ed at (818) 621-2570.[4]

---

4   Certified Financial Planner (CFP®), Chartered Financial Consultant (ChFC), Chartered Life Underwriter (CLU)

978-0-595-46742-6
0-595-46742-3

Printed in the United States
130615LV00001B/40/P